DEAR ALLIES

A STORY OF WOMEN IN MONKLANDS & BESIEGED LENINGRAD

by MARGARET HENDERSON

TO MY MOTHER

Published by Monklands District Libraries
ISBN 0946 120 218

The author acknowledges the assistance of:
Margaret Mudrak, Secretary of the Leningrad Branch of the USSR-Great
Britain Society.
The following members of the Leningrad Branch of the USSR-Great Britain
Society:
I. Podgorny
Belta Dianova
Tatiana Kuzmicheva
Katya Merchanskaya
Elena Berezantseva
Ludmila Stanukinas
Fanny Barnofskaya

George McAlister, Vice-President of the Scotland-USSR Society.
John Sams, General Secretary of the Scotland-USSR Society.
Kupava Birkett, translator.
Martin Dewhirst, The Department of Slavonic Languages and Literatures,
Glasgow University.
Professor John Erickson, Department of Defence Studies, Edinburgh
University.
Dr. Margaret Mackay, the School of Scottish Studies, Edinburgh University.
Provost Edward Cairns, Monklands District Council.
Eric J. Murray – Photographer.
The Chief Librarian and staff of Monklands District Library Services
Department.
The Director of Libraries and staff of Glasgow District Libraries.
Novosti Press Agency for use of photographs.
The Imperial War Museum for use of photographs.

INTRODUCTION

The Leningrad Album arrived in Scotland in 1943 when the people of Leningrad were entering the third year of the longest siege in modern history – starving and relentlessly bombed and shelled to satisfy Hitler's determination to break their will and to bring about the surrender of the city he was unable to capture, the city which bore the name of the founder of the Soviet Union.

The album was a work of art, sent by women in the besieged city in reply to an album containing messages of encouragement and admiration signed by several thousand women in two small towns in the West of Scotland, Airdrie and Coatbridge.

Shortly after its arrival in January 1943, the Leningrad Album was shown to the women of Airdrie and Coatbridge and then taken for safe keeping to the largest public reference library in Scotland, the Mitchell Library in Glasgow.

The Leningrad Album was not again officially exhibited to the people of Airdrie and Coatbridge until more than 40 years had passed, but it was not forgotten by one man who made regular pilgrimages from Airdrie, where he lived, to Glasgow to turn its pages – Harry Walker the only survivor of the group which initiated the Airdrie and Coatbridge Album in 1941, a modest gift to which the Leningrad Album was a magnificent response.

In 1985 the 40th anniversary of the end of the Second World War was commemorated. In that year there were two local events of interest in Airdrie and Coatbridge which by that time had been amalgamated into the district of Monklands; in Airdrie, the annual Visual Arts Exhibition and in Coatbridge an exhibition commemorating the centenary of its inauguration as a burgh.

Harry Walker suggested that the Leningrad Album should be on show at both exhibitions and the Provost of Monklands, Edward Cairns, and the Chief Executive of Monklands, Mr James Ness, warmly welcomed the idea.

Over the same period the author had been researching, independently of these initiatives, the story of the exchange of albums. She had learned of the existence of the two albums quite by chance, on a visit to Leningrad in 1984. At Friendship House in Leningrad where foreign visitors are welcomed, the 40th anniversary of the lifting of the Siege was being commemorated. The Grand Hall of Friendship House – the Shuvalov Palace in Tsarist times – was filled with school children, gathered to watch a film of the war and to listen to one of the stories of the Siege, told by Kira Ingal, deputy director of school no. 61 in Leningrad. It was a complete co-incidence that the author chose to join the schoolchildren and heard for the first time the story of the albums which Kira Ingal had researched and kept alive in Leningrad.

The interest and affection for the Leningrad Album shown by thousands of people in Monklands who inspected the album in 1985 led Monklands District Council to undertake publication of this book and to seek formal twinning links with the historic town of Gatchina near Leningrad, whose people also suffered greatly during the war, through enemy occupation.

The author offers this tribute to the memory of the victims of the Siege and to the survivors of the Siege with hopes that the generations succeeding them in Leningrad will know only the stories, but never the realities of war; that they may always live in peace and in friendship with their "dear allies" of 1941 to 1944.

MIR I DRUZHBA!

Peace and Friendship

Margaret Henderson

CONTENTS

Chapter 1

Early in the morning of June 22nd 1941, a Sunday, Adolf Hitler unleashed against the Soviet Union a military invasion on a scale unknown in the history of human conflict.

There was no declaration of war. At 3 a.m. a mechanised and armoured horde of three and a half million men of the German Wehrmacht with their Axis allies poured across the frontier while planes of the Luftwaffe rained down bombs on the sleeping border towns.

It was 5.45 a.m., British time, when Dr. Josef Goebbels, the German Minister for Propaganda, read the Fuhrer's proclamation: "The greatest march the world has ever seen is taking place."

The invasion was code-named Operation Barbarossa. Before it was a day old, more than a thousand planes of the Soviet Air Force had been destroyed before they could become airborne, such was the speed and devastating efficiency of the blitzkrieg – the 'lightning warfare' perfected by the Germans.

In the initial stages, the German forces were advancing at the rate of thirty miles a day and Operation Barbarossa was even ahead of schedule, a situation that was very satisfactory for Hitler and, in fact, just what he had envisaged after his earlier successes in Europe.

On 9th April 1940 the blitzkrieg had defeated Denmark in a single day. In the following eleven weeks it had brought about the capitulation of Norway, the Netherlands, Luxembourg, Belgium and France. Similar victories in the Balkan campaigns of early 1941 had given Germany possession of all the combatant nations of northern and eastern Europe. Of the Allied countries, Britain alone was undefeated in spite of heavy losses at sea, desperate air battles and prolonged Nazi bombing of industrial and civilian targets. Britain and the Soviet Union now stood together as the only countries resisting Nazi Germany.

The German attack on the Soviet Union was three-pronged. Army Group South was to aim for the oilfields and the fertile farmlands of the Ukraine. Army Group Centre's objective was the capture of Moscow. The thirty divisions of Army Group North, supported by 430 aircraft of the First Air Fleet were to over-run the Baltic States and enter Leningrad, the city Hitler called "the breeding centre of Bolshevism".

To the people of Leningrad their city was the cradle of three workers' revolutions and the city named after Lenin, where the founder of the Soviet state had announced the birth of the world's first Socialist society in 1917.

Defenders of Leningrad

Constructed as the Tsar Peter the Great's dream of a capital city, Leningrad had been embellished and cherished for more than two centuries. It was no longer the administrative capital, but it remained the brilliant centre of culture and learning it had been since its foundation in 1703.

As the Nazi war machine advanced, the Soviet people learned that the wanton destruction and brutality against civilians for which the Wehrmacht was already famous were being practised with a much greater zeal than in other countries. German War propaganda had long reflected Hitler's contempt for Communism and the 'Slavs', as he called all the peoples of the Soviet Union.

As Army Group North came closer, Leningraders feared for their lovely city as much as they feared for themselves and their children. In the first two weeks of the invasion, an even higher percentage of civilians in Leningrad than elsewhere in the Soviet Union volunteered for the Opolcheniye – The People's Army.

Carrying pickaxes and shovels they left the city in their thousands; women, old men, boys and girls. By the end of July almost a million citizens were helping the Red Army units to prepare for the invader by the construction of hundreds of miles of triple defence lines. By the time the people of Leningrad had done what they could to protect their city, 15,875 miles of trenches and 340 miles of anti-tank ditches had been dug by hand and more than 400 miles of barbed-wire defences and 5,000 firing points had been erected.

By the middle of August, Army Group North had come to a halt within firing distance of Leningrad. The people were back in the city, working night and day on anti-tank barricades in the streets and firing points in their own homes and laying mines which would blow up their most treasured buildings at the approach of the enemy in case they should all perish from hunger.

As Autumn approached it seemed that this would indeed be their fate. By early September the city was surrounded and almost three million people were trapped, more than half a million of them children. The Siege of Leningrad had begun. In the nine hundred days before it was lifted almost a million citizens were to die of starvation, yet not a single German soldier crossed the city boundaries, except as a prisoner of war at the end of the Siege.

Anti-tank barriers on the outskirts of Leningrad.

Women building defences in the streets of Leningrad

13

Chapter 2

"When Operation Barbarossa is launched the world will hold its breath" Hitler had boasted. He was right! But in Britain, astonishment at his audacity was quickly replaced by feelings of a profound admiration for the Soviet Union and calls for solidarity.

On the evening after the invasion Winston Churchill made an emotional speech on radio. His words must have surprised listeners more familiar with the anti-Communist rhetoric he had employed since the Revolution of 1917 when he had talked of 'strangling the infant Bolshevism in its cradle'.

"I see the Russian soldiers standing on the threshold of their native land" he said, "I see advancing in hideous onslaught the Nazi war machine. We shall give whatever help we can to Russia and the Russian people. We shall appeal to our friends and allies in every part of the world to take the same course and pursue it, as we shall, faithfully and steadfastly to the end. Russia's danger is our danger and the danger of the United States, just as the cause of any Russian fighting for his hearth and home is the cause of free men and free people in every corner of the globe."

As far as the British people were concerned, Churchill's exhortations proved to be hardly necessary. The unity of purpose that had swept Britain during the German bombing of civilian targets and the threatened invasion of Britain simply found a new direction when Hitler turned eastwards. People of all social classes and political persuasions were united in grief for the agony of the Soviet Union and gratitude for the gallant resistance of Red Army soldiers and civilian defenders. All over Britain Tanks for Russia weeks were held when an entire week's production in munitions factories was earmarked for the Eastern Front.

All over Britain groups were set up to raise funds for the Soviet war effort. One of the largest was the British Red Cross for Russia Fund headed by Winston Churchill's wife, Clementine Churchill.

'Mrs. Churchill's Fund', as the public called it, received donations of more than a million pounds in its first three months.

"We in Britain were filled with admiration at the heroic resistance put up by the men and women – even the children – of the USSR," Mrs. Churchill explained later, "We wanted to flash a signal of comradeship across the wastes of subjugated Europe. Our hearts were with the Russian soldiers and the civilian population of the over-run territories."

The first reports of the appalling hardships suffered by the defenders of Leningrad touched a special chord in British hearts. When Leningrad was

Tanks for the Soviet Union

Savings Poster Trafalgar Square London.

Come into the factories

surrounded, there was a feeling of helplessness as well as outrage. Then communications were cut off and it became clear that Hitler, having failed to take the city by direct attack, had decided on a slow starvation of the population, which he imagined – but he could not have been more mistaken - would bring about surrender.

In Airdrie and Coatbridge,[1] contributions for the Eastern Front were generous. Many men, in an area where the unemployment rate had been high since the Depression had found jobs, after years out of work, in factories converted to war production. Many women were also in paid jobs outside the home for the first time in their lives. In Airdrie there was a Russia Today Society. The women in the Society were keen to help the Russian war effort in any way they could since many of them were mothers of young children and therefore unable to contribute directly to the British war effort by going out to work.

On the committee of the Russia Today Society was Mrs Agnes Maxwell the mother of a ten year old son, Alex and a daughter, Jenny, four years of age. In October 1941 the committee met in Cullen Street, Airdrie, in an endeavour to find some way of expressing the admiration for the Soviet resistance, and especially for the people of the besieged city of Leningrad. Other members of the committee were Agnes's husband Harry Maxwell, Harry Walker, William O'Byrne, Peter Creegan and Margaret Plant, an art teacher.

Harry Walker, from Airdrie, the only surviving member of that committee, recalled the discussion on that auspicious evening:

"The eyes of the world were on Leningrad and we were all aware of the tremendous contribution of women volunteers defending the city, night and day, against the Fascist forces."

"We had a large and enthusiastic women's section in the Russia Today Society in Airdrie. All the women were deeply affected by what they had been hearing about women in Leningrad. They were also desperately anxious to do something to feel part of the vast struggle that was taking place."

"The plight of Leningrad was the sole topic of discussion at that committee meeting. We agreed to act immediately, for we could not know how long the besieged city would hold out, the situation was so grave. We decided that a collection of women's signatures should be made in Airdrie and in the neighbouring town of Coatbridge and somehow sent to the women of Leningrad with a message conveying our admiration and feelings of solidarity."

---

[1] Airdrie and Coatbridge are adjacent towns in the West of Scotland, near Glasgow. In 1975 these two towns, together with a large section of rural North Lanarkshire were amalgamated to form Monklands District.

Harry Walker

The committee's next decision was to set up in Airdrie and Coatbridge two Housewives' Organisations of women volunteers who would collect signatures and other messages in both towns. Approaches were to be made to all local women's organisations, youth groups, churches and cooperative societies. Agnes Maxwell was elected chairman of the Airdrie Housewives' Organisation.

Agnes Maxwell was born in 1905 in Airdrie, as Agnes Sarah Fraser Black. She had one sister and four brothers, two of whom became professional footballers. Richard Black played for three clubs – Morton, Manchester City and St. Mirren – and later became a groundsman for Airdrieonians. William played for Airdrieonians, Hibernian and Watford and, after the 2nd World War, for Dunfermline Athletic.

Agnes Maxwell's first job after leaving school was in Hunter's flower shop in Airdrie. She then went into what was then called 'service', working as a maid in a town in the East of Scotland, but conditions were hard and she was not happy in the job. She returned to Airdrie and married Harry Maxwell in 1928. Influenced by her husband she developed an interest in politics that lasted throughout her life.

Harry Maxwell, born in 1897, was brought up in Johnston Street, Airdrie and educated at Albert School. Two of his brothers who volunteered for army service when the First World War broke out were killed in action, Willie Maxwell who served in the Argyll and Sutherland Highlanders and Robert Maxwell who was in the Highland Light Infantry. Willie was killed at the Battle of the Somme and Robert at Gallipoli. Another brother Alex, known as Sanny, was also in the Argyll and Sutherlands. Harry Maxwell himself served with the Enniskillen Fusiliers. Among them the brothers were awarded ten medals.

At the age of twenty one, Harry Maxwell returned to the deprivation and unemployment which blighted the lives of so many families in the West of Scotland between the two world wars.

His son, Alex Maxwell, believed that it was probably his father's disillusion-ment with unemployment and post-war poverty that led to his interest in politics. He found work in various factories – each of them closed down – and finally at the Tube Works in Airdrie where he was a prominent activist during the General Strike of 1926. The tubeworks closed in 1928 and he remained unemployed until the outbreak of the 2nd World War.

Shortly after their marriage Agnes and Harry Maxwell were taking part in the 'hunger marches', a regular form of protest by the unemployed in Britain during the 1920s and 1930s. Harry Maxwell was the organiser of the contingent from Airdrie which took part in a walk from Glasgow to Edinburgh. In 1931 Mr and Mrs Maxwell both joined the Airdrie branch of the Communist Party founded in 1930 and together they helped to raise funds for the Aid to

Spain campaign which sent food and medical supplies to Spain during the Spanish Civil War. They also kept in touch with local volunteers who fought with the republicans in the Civil War.

The Maxwells brought up their two children in a 'single end' (a room and kitchen) in a lane off Aitchison Street, Airdrie until they were allocated a council house at 19 Park Crescent, Whinhall in 1939.

Work was not hard to find as preparations for war began. When hostilities broke out, like many more unemployed men in Britain, Harry Maxwell had a choice of jobs for the first time in his life and he worked throughout the war. Agnes Maxwell remained at home, looking after her husband and children, her father, a widower, and an evacuee from Birmingham, a boy about her son's age. But she still made time for outside activities.

"I can imagine how wholeheartedly my mother would throw herself into the task of collecting signatures for the women of Leningrad" said Alex Maxwell. "Although she had a very busy domestic life, she was never the sort of woman to confine her activities to the home. She was well-organised, determined and reliable. I suppose she was an unusual women in her day, dedicated to politics and an equal partner in her marriage. My mother and father were comrades in every sense of the word."

Harry Walker remembered that there was no difficulty in finding volunteers from the women who joined the housewives' organisations to call at factories and knock on doors for signatures. Some of the women would put the baby in the pram and call at houses in their own neighbourhood. Others dressed toddlers in warm coats when the older children had left for school and headed for the housing schemes. There was no time to lose. The news filtering through from Leningrad horrified all who read it. Besides, in Scotland the winter days were getting shorter and in the 'black-outs' of the war years there was no street lighting in Britain.

The women called at the Imperial Shell Plant; the Sun Foundry; the Calder Works in Coatbridge; the Lanarkshire Steel Works. At the SMT Aircraft factory in Carlisle Road, Airdrie 500 women signed. At the Airdrie Rivet, Nut and Bolt works, 150 women, describing themselves proudly as "industrial war workers". added their names and addresses. The local newspaper the Airdrie and Coatbridge Advertiser reported that "every factory in both towns was visited". Mrs. Agnes Tennent, the wife of Provost James Tennent of Coatbridge agreed that her name should head the list of individual signatures. The Tennents lived at Beechwood, Airdrie and Mrs. Tennent was the organiser of the Women's Voluntary Service in Coatbridge. Another signature was that of Mrs. David Gray, whose husband was Provost of Airdrie.

"I know that not a single woman invited to sign her name refused" Harry Walker recalled "A few husbands added their names and some of the women collecting signatures had donations pressed into their hands on doorsteps with a request that the money should be used for the relief of suffering on the Eastern Front."

Every organisation approached responded to the appeal.

The message from the women of Greenhill Knitting Circle in Coatbridge was typical of the messages from local organisations:

Dear Women of Leningrad,

We are glad of this opportunity of expressing our gratitude to your country and our admiration of the terrific battle you are waging against our common foe, the enemy of all progress and humanity.

We are horrified at the suffering brought on the people of Europe by fascism but we know that Britain and Russia and America together will eventually defeat this fascist horror. Fighting together we can do it.

The women here will "do our own bit" to the best of our ability and we look forward with you to the time when we shall build a new world of peace and goodwill amongst men and women the world over.

With our best wishes to our splendid ally.

Chapter 3

The volume of messages and signatures collected was much greater than had been expected. Agnes Maxwell and her helpers met to consider the best way to put them together before sending them off to Leningrad. It was Margaret Plant who thought of creating an album to contain the sheets on which the messages and names were written. As the only artist on the committee, she was invited to undertake the illustration and binding of the album – the Airdrie and Coatbridge Album, as it was eventually called.

For the cover of the album, she chose a local tartan, the Buchanan, as background and added the thistle, Scotland's national emblem with a quotation from Robert Burns.

Margaret Plant was born in 1901 in Coatbridge. Her mother was from the Marshall family, the owners of Marshalls the bootmakers which had branches in Airdrie, Coatbridge and Falkirk. Her father was a bricklayer who repaired and re-lined furnaces – a highly skilled job.

She was brought up in a semi-detatched villa in Gartsherrie Road with her three brothers. When she graduated from Glasgow School of Art, teaching posts were scarce and she taught art part-time at St Mary's, Whifflet, Coatbridge and at Albert School, Airdrie until the outbreak of war when more posts became vacant as male teachers were called up to the forces. Her first full-time job was in the art department of St John's Secondary School, Hamilton.

Mrs Marion Lang of Espieside Crescent, Coatbridge was friendly with Margaret Plant for 40 years. "We first met in 1920" she recalled "We were both in the Girl Guide company attached to Old Monkland Church."

After the First World War, Margaret Plant began to take an interest in radical politics like many others in the area at the time. She joined the Communist Party in the mid-1930s, organising women's sections throughout Lanarkshire.

Marion Lang remembered Margaret Plant taking part in fund-raising for Russia in Coatbridge – "Sales of work and auctions were organised locally and people were out in the streets with cans, collecting for Russia. It was quite common to see passers-by stuffing a £1 note in a can – and that was a big sum of money in those days."

"I suppose most of the workers in the munitions factories were taking home wages much bigger than in peace time. But even families with men away at the war and with less money to spare were still generous when they heard the collection was for the Soviet Union."

"Margaret was teaching full-time then and the streets were dark by the time she came out of school but she managed to collect hundreds of signatures for Leningrad. Women would stop her in the street. The word had gone round, you see, and everyone wanted to sign. She called at factories – everybody was working overtime then and in some factories so many women wanted to sign that she left the message and sheets of paper with the foreman and returned next day to collect them so that production wouldn't be interrupted."

For a' that, and a' that,
It's comin' yet, for a' that,
That man to man, the warld o'er,
Shall brothers be for a' that!
Robert Burns.

GREETINGS
TO THE
WOMEN
OF
LENINGRAD

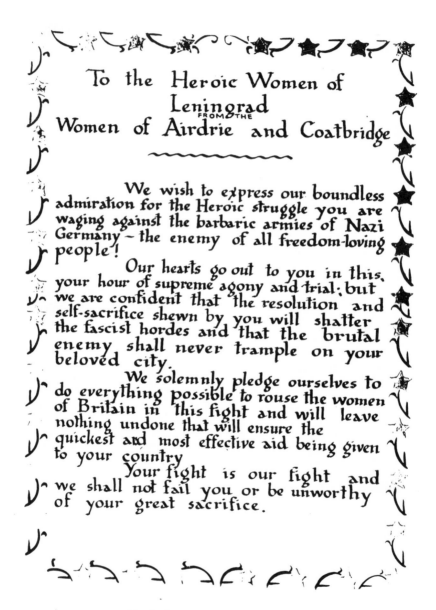

To the Heroic Women of Leningrad
FROM THE
Women of Airdrie and Coatbridge

We wish to express our boundless admiration for the Heroic struggle you are waging against the barbaric armies of Nazi Germany – the enemy of all freedom-loving people!

Our hearts go out to you in this, your hour of supreme agony and trial; but we are confident that the resolution and self-sacrifice shewn by you will shatter the fascist hordes and that the brutal enemy shall never trample on your beloved city.

We solemnly pledge ourselves to do everything possible to rouse the women of Britain in this fight and will leave nothing undone that will ensure the quickest and most effective aid being given to your country

Your fight is our fight and we shall not fail you or be unworthy of your great sacrifice.

"To the heroic women of Leningrad"

This is our Town – Airdrie

This is our Town – Coatbridge

St: Thomas Church
Coatbridge.

We...the women of "The Bright Hour" of St Thomas Church.. wish to send you a warm hand of fellowship in these days of great trial...and to tell you how much we admire the great-hearted courage with which you are meeting these difficult times.

Week by week we pray for you to The Great God Who loves courage and heroism wherever it is found... asking Him to comfort..strengthen and protect you and all you love.

St. Thomas Church Coatbridge

The Airdrie and Coatbridge Album contains a poem celebrating the anniversary of the birth of Robert Burns written by Janet Hamilton, a local poetess.

Born in 1795, Janet Hamilton was the daughter of James Thomson, an agricultural labourer on the home farm of Drumpellier Estate who later opened his own shoemaker's shop opposite the Old Monkland Parish School, Coatbridge. She taught herself and her ten children to read and at the age of 54 she taught herself to write and began contributing to a magazine called Cassels Working Man's Friend. She never travelled more than 10 miles from her home in the village of Langloan but she read the works of Shakespeare, Milton, Fergusson, and Burns, corresponded with Harriet Beecher Stowe, the author of Uncle Tom's Cabin, and had a visit from the son of the Italian patriot, Garribaldi. She died in 1873 aged 78. Her grave is in the Old Monkland Churchyard and on her tombstone are inscribed the words: 'She being dead yet speaketh'.

As Margaret Plant stayed up late at night putting the finishing touches to the decoration of the album, requests to sign it were still coming in. Agnes Maxwell was obliged to put a notice in the Airdrie and Coatbridge Advertiser announcing the closure of the appeal for signatures:

The deputation of housewives will leave for London on Friday night and will be accorded a reception at the Soviet Embassy on Saturday afternoon.

The number of women wishing to send greetings has been so great that extra pages have had to be added to the album.

Should there be other women who would like to add a message, they are asked to communicate with Mrs Agnes Maxwell at 19 Park Crescent, Airdrie, without delay.

Women's organisations and youth groups attached to churches of all denominations – Roman Catholic, Church of Scotland, Baptist, Methodist, Congregational – had contributed messages to the album. Probably the last church to do so was the West Parish Church, Airdrie. The President of the Women's Guild wrote to Agnes Maxwell on 19th December 1941.

Dear Mrs Maxwell,

The Women's Guild of the West Parish Church, Airdrie, at its meeting today unanimously agreed to send a message to the women of Leningrad. If it is not too late, could you put it in the album?
The message followed:
To the women of Leningrad:
We admire your courage
We sympathise with your suffering
We pray for your complete victory.

In two weeks, more than 6000 signatures had been added to the messages of love and support to be sent from the women of Airdrie and Coatbridge with their hopes and prayers that they would cross the enemy lines safely – and above all, that they would reach their Soviet sisters before it was too late.

Harry Walker believed that the name of every woman, every organisation, and every church in both towns would have appeared in the lists, had events not set a time limit to the project:-

"Hitler was boasting that the swastika instead of the hammer and sickle would fly in Leningrad and Moscow by Christmas. The lists had to be closed."

CHAPTER 4

December 1941 was the worst month of the whole war for the people of Leningrad – the winter was the coldest for a hundred years, deaths from starvation were reaching 4000 a day. It was clear that the album could be kept no longer. The housewives' organisations had already written for advice from the Soviet Embassy in London on its despatch and Madame Agnes Maisky, the wife of the Soviet Ambassador, Ivan Maisky, had replied promising to do all she could to get the album to Leningrad and suggesting that they could deliver it to her personally at the Embassy.

Madame Maisky's name was already well-known to the women who were to be presented to her. They had heard her appeals on radio for all possible help for her motherland, read about her visits to factories all over Britain and her friendship with Mrs. Churchill. They had seen photographs of her in the newspapers attending fund-raising galas in London with her husband.

On Thursday 11th December 1941, a gathering described in the Airdrie and Coatbridge Advertiser as a "send-off" meeting for the album was held in the Sir John Wilson Town Hall, Airdrie.

Margaret Plant had been invited to hand over the album to Agnes Maxwell who was leading the deputation leaving for London the next day. On the evening before the function, Mrs Lang received a message asking her to call at Margaret Plant's home:

"Margaret wanted me to take her place at the presentation. She wasn't feeling too well and I sensed, although she didn't say so, that she was probably suffering from a bit of 'stage fright' too. I knew her well enough to understand that to be the focus of attention at such a large gathering would be an ordeal for her. She was such a modest, retiring person."

"We had a last look at the album together. Some of the pages listing the names of factory workers were smudged with grime from the women's hands. We got a rubber and did the best we could to clean it up a bit before it left on its long journey.

"I was on my way out when a thought struck me: Did you sign it yourself?" I said. "I was right, she hadn't. She'd been too busy running around getting other people's names to think about herself."

On Saturday 13th December Agnes Maxwell and four other members of the housewives' organisation met Madame Maisky at the Soviet Embassy in London. They represented the thousands of women in Airdrie and Coatbridge who had written their names in the album. When the album was handed over

Madame Maisky christens a Valentine Tank

with a bouquet of flowers, Madame Maisky expressed her profound gratitude.

As the Airdrie and Coatbridge Advertiser reported "She told the deputation that the album was one of the finest tributes she had received and the first of its kind from Scotland. Then, prompted by the five Scottish women, she read aloud the quotation from Burns. She spoke about Russia's struggle and gave each of her visitors an autographed book and a pamphlet."

"Tea was then served with what Madame Maisky believed to be 'Scottish scones.' No offence was taken when the members of the deputation enlightened the ambassador's wife. On the contrary, she was most interested to learn about the authentic Scottish method of baking girdle scones."

On Sunday 14th December, Mrs Maxwell was invited to speak at a meeting for the promotion of Anglo-Soviet Unity in Hampstead, North London, at which the Mayor of Hampstead presided. In her speech Mrs Maxwell gave the audience details of what was being done in this respect in Airdrie and Coatbridge. After the meeting the Mayor asked her to take back the message to Airdrie and Coatbridge that in Hampstead they were "straining every nerve to bring about Anglo-Soviet unity."

Shortly after their return to Scotland each member of the deputation received a letter of thanks from Madame Maisky.

I would like to say how much I appreciated your visit here and getting to know about all that you have been doing in Airdrie and Coatbridge to help my country. I greatly appreciate the desire of all of you to demonstrate your unity with us in this great struggle in which all freedom-loving nations are now engaged, against a common enemy. The main danger is still from Hitlerite Germany and this calls for the closest unity and collaboration of our peoples in order to bring about the complete and final defeat of the fascist hordes.

I therefore welcome the efforts of all those who are doing so much to achieve this end.

With all good wishes,
Yours sincerely,

Agnes Maisky.

The members of the deputation representing the women of Airdrie and Coatbridge had been deeply touched when Madame Maisky had given them hope of a reply to their message of encouragement to the women of Leningrad, but they felt a reply was more than they had the right to expect, in the circumstances. It was enough, surely, that the album had been honoured with official recognition, which meant that every effort would be made to get it to its destination.

Agnes Maxwell and her companions returned to Scotland and were soon busy with preparations for another 'austerity' Christmas. As the struggle against Fascism continued unabated for the Soviet Union and Britain, Agnes Maxwell continued with her work for the local war effort.

She had been elected secretary of the Airdrie branch of the Women's Anglo-Soviet Committee and she was active in collections for the National Anglo-Soviet Medical Aid Fund. She was to continue fund-raising for medical aid to Russia until 1943 when a bed was endowed in Stalingrad City Clinical Hospital, bearing a plaque with the inscription: "From the People of Airdrie."

In 1942, there were plenty of good causes on the 'home front' too and Agnes Maxwell supported three of them. She organised appeals for blood donors for British soldiers wounded in the Far East and North Africa; she helped to raise money, for the Prisoners of War Relatives' Fund, and she campaigned for 'war nurseries' for the children of women working in local factories.

At the beginning of June 1942, a telegram from the Soviet Union arrived in Airdrie. It was delivered in its brown envelope to 19 Park Cresent, addressed to Mrs. Agnes Maxwell. It contained a message from the Anti-Fascist Committee of Soviet Women in Leningrad.

For more than forty years, the excitement surrounding the arrival of that telegram remained one of the most vivid recollections of Harry Walker's life :

"It was like something from another world, a miracle. It was just unbelievable that the women of Leningrad, struggling with hunger and disease and face-to-face with death, should find the time to respond to our pledge of solidarity and admiration."

"News of the telegram from Leningrad spread from house to house like wildfire. A meeting of women concerned with the album was arranged immediately and I attended it, with the other members of the committee of the Russia Today Society."

"Agnes Maxwell arrived with the telegram and it was read aloud, then passed from hand to hand. We couldn't believe our eyes. Some of us wept with joy as we read the message:"

"Your greeting was received by the women of Leningrad with great enthusiasim. It was read at meetings attended by women workers, teachers, scientists and housewives. The text of a message in reply to Scotland was unanimously adopted at those meetings."

A message in reply? A message from the committee . . . perhaps a letter of thanks? Was it realistic to expect any further news? The women of Leningrad had received the album and that was the important thing.

During the war, wives and mothers everywhere tended to live from day to day, keeping busy and trying not to build up hopes which would only make disappointments or bad news harder to bear.

When 1942 ended and another year of war began, there was still no message, but the news was better from the Leningrad Front.

On 18th January 1943, a desperate counter attack by the Red Army defenders of Leningrad had been partially successful. It had broken through the enemy lines and created a narrow corridor through which supplies could reach the city. Some evacuation from Leningrad was also possible through this narrow 'Corridor of Death' which was under constant shelling and frequent dive bombing attacks.

On 30th January 1943, a notice appeared in the Airdrie and Coatbridge Advertiser, announcing an expected visit by Madame Maisky to the West of Scotland. According to wartime practice, the precise date was not made public for reasons of national security. It was to be "sometime next week."

The report added: "It is hoped that she might be able to include Airdrie and Coatbridge in her visit. What gives rise to this hope is that there has arrived an album which the women of Leningrad are sending to women of Airdrie and Coatbridge in reply to the album sent there last year."

Neither Airdrie nor Coatbridge were in fact visited by Madame Maisky. It seems that the Ministry of Information in London had arranged her itinerary under the misapprehension that the album contained signatures and messages from women in Glasgow.

Only through the speedy intervention of Agnes Maxwell were Airdrie and Coatbridge women represented at the ceremony arranged for the presentation of the album – at the City Chambers in Glasgow. Two days before the report appeared about the impending visit of the Ambassador's wife, Agnes Maxwell had written in her capacity as secretary of the Womens' Anglo-Soviet Committee to advise the embassy of the ministerial error.

19 Park Crescent,
Airdrie,
Scotland.

28th January 1943.

Madame Maisky,
Soviet Embassy,
13 Kensington Gardens,
London.

Dear Madame Maisky,

I have just been at the Ministry of Information re your visit to Scotland. I have been led to understand that you were presenting an Album to the Women of Airdrie and Coatbridge from the Women of Leningrad and they informed me that the Album is being presented to the Women of Glasgow. I am afraid there is some mistake here as I was informed a few weeks ago that an album had left Leningrad and to be on the look-out for it.

A year ago I personally delivered to the Soviet Embassy an Album from the women of Airdrie and Coatbridge and I would like to hear from you, by telegram, if possible, if you are scheduled for Airdrie or Coatbridge so that I can make the necessary arrangements.

Yours sincerely,

Agnes Maxwell
Secretary
Anglo-Soviet Committee

The ceremony went ahead as the Ministry of Information had planned it, but the members of the deputation of women who had taken the first album to London more than a year earlier were invited. Also present were, according to the Airdrie and Coatbridge Advertiser, "women war workers and representatives of local women's organisations."

As Madame Maisky handed over the album to the wife of the Lord Provost of Glasgow, Mrs. J. M. Biggar, she apologised for the delay and paid tribute, "among great applause from the audience", to the women of Leningrad.

"Women in Leningrad" she said, "have replaced the men in factories. They have cleared away the wreckage of bombed buildings, kept the streets clear of snow, nursed the wounded and buried the dead."

"We ask you to do your utmost to see that in close friendship with us, victory over our common enemy will be achieved as soon as possible."

Madame Maisky was accompanied by Lieutenant-Commander V. Voronin of the USSR Navy. Her other engagements in Scotland included a visit to the Russian Bookshop in Glasgow, to a "Clyde shipyard" and a "West of Scotland war factory" where an impromptu collection yielded almost £90 for Russian relief funds.

Madame Maisky had lunch with the Lord Provost of Glasgow who told her that a football used in the recent "Old Firm" match between Rangers and Celtic, traditionally held on New Year's Day, was to be auctioned in aid of the Stalingrad fund.

Newsprint was scarce in Britain in 1943 but the Glasgow Herald gave ample coverage to the gathering, even describing what Madame Maisky was wearing – a black astrakhan coat with matching hat over a heather coloured woollen suit.

That evening Agnes Maxwell's voice was heard on BBC Radio. A short speech she had made at the function in the City Chambers was recorded after the 6 o'clock news. Mrs Maxwell had also proposed the vote of thanks to Madame Maisky, deputising for the Duchess of Atholl who had been taken ill.

It was decided that the Leningrad Album should be kept in Glasgow as a tribute to women all over Scotland who had demonstrated concern, in various ways, for their Soviet allies. To reach the widest possible public, it was to be on show at the Kelvingrove Museum and Art Galleries in Glasgow at the same time as an exhibition on the contribution of Soviet young people to the defence of their homeland. Then it was to become the property of the Mitchell Library in Glasgow.

But first it was shown to the people of Airdrie and Coatbridge.

(Mrs Maxwell examining Leningrad Album)

On 6th February 1943, Madame Maisky wrote to Agnes Maxwell informing her that she had personally written to the Lord Provost of Glasgow asking him to arrange to send the album for exhibition in the area where it had been created, "so that all organisations may see the greetings sent to them from Leningrad in their own locality."

The last week of February 1943 was designated "Russia Week" in Airdrie and the centrepiece of an exhibition at the Sir John Wilson Town Hall was the album from Leningrad.

It was a splendid exhibition with several hundred photographs depicting the history and culture of the Soviet Union, Red Army heroes and the Red Army in training. A display of 50 more photographs was devoted to British-Soviet unity describing "mutual efforts to reach a common end."

As thousands of citizens of Airdrie and Coatbridge filed past the album, the Red Flag of the Soviet Union, flew over Airdrie Town Hall, as a tribute to the people whose steadfast and selfless resistance to the enemy threatening civilisation itself had won the respect of the entire free world.

Harry Walker was there :
"Sadness and tears" he remembered, "mingled with joy and happiness as the pages of the album were turned, as its beauty was revealed and the feelings of friendship and solidarity it represented were transferred to all who passed by. Many were visibly affected as they examined this unique gift to the people of Airdrie and Coatbridge. Many were heard to remark on the need to speed up the opening of a Second Front to hasten the final defeat of the German Army."

CHAPTER 5
– THE LENINGRAD ALBUM.

DEAR ALLIES. –

To the women of Airdrie and Coatbridge.

We have been moved to the depths of our souls by the words of love and greeting from those distanced from us in far-off Scotland. We thank you for the help you are giving us in the struggle with Hitler's Germany. While there is Hitlerism, there is suffering and death – this is the lot of women. Our husbands and brothers are cut off from us, our homes are in danger, our children are doomed to destruction or bondage.

The women of Leningrad, just like the women of Airdrie and Coatbridge, have risen to the defence of their homes, their honour, their independence and their freedom. The ungovernable hatred for the common enemy and the struggle to have revenge on the fascist barbarians for all our suffering fills our hearts.

We are proud that we have such a worthy ally as the people of Great Britain.

The treaty concluded between our countries on the 26th May 1942 will give us new strength in the battle with the German aggressors. Rendering one another military assistance and the support of each country in the war with Germany and her allies in Europe we are coming closer to the not too-far-distant time when our just cause will win a complete victory.

Dear Allies, we have much! Women are a great strength. It is up to us to hasten this victory.

We shall do everything to ensure that the year 1942 will be the year of the final rout of Hitler's armies, the year of liberation of all humanity from the bloodstained nightmare which is Hitlerism!

Statue of Lenin which stands in front of the Smolnyy Institute, Leningrad.

Смольный

ЛЕНИНГРАД

SMOLNY INSTITUTE, LENINGRAD

Дорогие друзья наши, —
Женщины Эйдри и Котбриджа!

Мы от имени души тронуты вашими любви и привета, Женщины книг из Великой Шотландии. Мы благодарим вас за помощь, которую вы нам оказываете в борьбе с немецкой Германией.

Пока существует литература, страдание и скорбь жёнщин, наших жён и братьев отрывают от нас, наши дети отрываются от себя или гибель.

Женщина, любящая, такие, как и женщина Эйдри и Котбриджа, поднялись на защиту своего очага, своей чести, независимости и свободы.

Некоторая любовь к обиду друг и стремление отомстить раз жизненной воеводой за все наши страдания, являются наши сердца.

Мы горды тем, что имеем так ...

со Смародного сотника, как является герб Вели-британии.

Вскоре, раскопанный нашими страшней 26 мая 1942 года, приблизил нам новые силы в борьбе с немецким германским ... нашими русскими войсками под Харьковом сражением в Сирии, как её сообщника в войне и сирийском ... приблизила то немецкой ... войне любые трудные дни одержат полную победу.

Дорогие наши сотрудники, как любо! женщины-сотрудники силы ... от нас зависит удержать эту победу.

Братель уже всё, чтобы 1942 год стал годом окончательного разгрома и прогнать грязной ... ненавистного человечества от рабства нас всего человечества от ... контроля, ненавистного Гитлером!

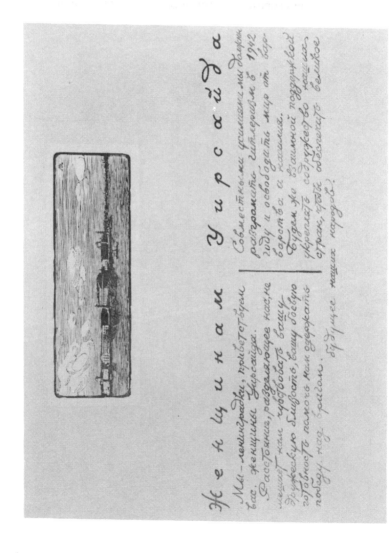

Женщинам Урала

Мы-ленинградцы, приветствуем вас, женщины Урала. Расстояние, разделяющее нас, не мешает нам чувствовать вашу трудовую близость, вашу боевую готовность всемя нам держать победу над врагом. Будущее наших народов...

Советскими руками мы завтра разгромим гитлеризм в 1942 году и освободим мир от варварства и насилия. Будем же взаимной поддержкой укреплять содружество наших стран, ради общего великого...

VIEW ACROSS THE RIVER NEVA FROM WINTER PALACE EMBANKMENT.

"The distance that separates us does not prevent us from feeling how close you are in friendship and your militant readiness to help us to overcome our enemies. We must vanquish Hitlerism by our joint efforts in 1942 and liberate the world from barbarism and violence. Let us by mutual support strengthen the co-operation of our countries to ensure a great future for our peoples."

Коммунистической партии Юрри.

женской секции.

Дорогие товарищи!

Мы, женщины Ленинграда – города, носящего имя великого ЛЕНИНА, сердечно приветствуем Вас и жмём Ваши руки.

В течение многих месяцев, вместе с частями Красной Армии, мы прилагали все усилия, чтобы не дать фашистским варварам взять любимый город Вдохновителя Сталина, мы закалялись в этой тяжелой борьбе. Наши силы растут с каждым днем. Ваше письмо ещё раз убеждает нас в том, что мы не одни, — с нами дружественные народы Великобритании и Америки и все

свободолюбивое, передовое челове=
чество.

Мы высоко ценим Ваше обязатель=
ство работать так, чтобы пол=
ностью нам обеспечить победу над фашизмом.

Не жалея сил, мы будем бороться за то, чтобы ни одного захватчи= ка не осталось на нашей земле.

1942 год будет стать годом разгрома немецких разбойни= ков, годом разгрома гитлеровцев. Вместе с Вами – под знаменем Маркса-Энгельса-Ленина-Сталина –вперёд, к победе!

SMOLNYY INSTITUTE.

To the Communist Party of Airdrie, Women's Section.

"Dear Comrades: We women of Leningrad, a city which bears the name of the great Lenin, send you our sincere greetings and shake you by the hand. For many months now, we and the units of the Red Army have been making all possible efforts to prevent the enemy from breaking into our beloved city. We are inspired and strengthened in this difficult struggle by Stalin. Our strength grows every day. Your letter once again convinced us that we are not alone. The friendly peoples of Great Britain and America and all freedom-loving and progressive mankind are with us. We very much appreciate your undertaking to work so as to help us speed up the victory over the enemy. We will not spare our strength and will fight to ensure that not one member of the German occupation forces remains in our country. 1942 must become the year in which the German invaders are defeated, the year in which Hitler is smashed. Together with you under the banner of Marx, Engels, Lenin and Stalin – forward to victory."

Девушкам Кот-Бриджа
от Девушек Ленинграда

Дорогие подруги!

THE ADMIRALTY.

To the girls of Airdrie from the girls of Leningrad

"Dear Friends: We send you our warm greetings. Your undertaking to help us found a warm echo in our hearts. Fascism hangs like a black cloud over our young lives. We do not spare our strength in the name of a splendid future and of life itself, to ensure victory over the hated and inexorable enemy. Hand in hand with you in this struggle, relying on the ever-strengthening unity and help of our states, we will fight for and achieve the right to freedom and happiness."

Женщинам Эйрдри

Дорогие сестры!
Мы тронуты дружеским выражением ваших чувств.
Ваши мысли о нас и ваша поддержка помогают нам стойко переносить все трудности борьбы с общим врагом.

Мы твердо верим, что, объединив наши с вами усилия, мы поможем разгрому гитлеровских орд в 1942 году.

ONE OF THE ROSTRAL COLUMNS.

"Dear sisters: We are moved by the friendly expression of your feelings, your thoughts about us and your support. Help us to be staunch in bearing all the difficulties of the fight against the common enemy. We firmly believe that by uniting our and your efforts we shall help to overcome the Hitlerite hordes in 1942."

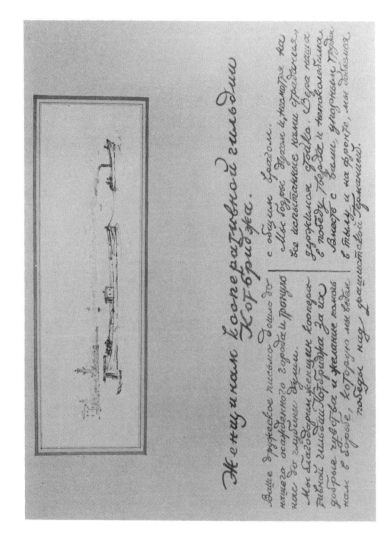

Женщинам Кооперативной гильдии Котбриджа.

Ваше дружеское письмо дошло до нашего осаждённого города и тронуло нас до глубины души.

Мы благодарим вас, дорогие работницы гильдии Котбриджа за их добрые чувства и желание помочь нам в борьбе, которую мы вели

с общим врагом...

Мы будем твёрдо и несмотря на все испытания наши уверены...

уверенные в победе. Будем и неколебимы в победу победе и понимаем

вместе с вами, упорным трудом в тылу и на фронте, мы создаём победу над фашистской Германией.

BARGE BEING PULLED ALONG THE NEVA.

To the women of the Co-operative Guild of Coatbridge

"Your friendly letter reached our besieged city and touched us to the depths of our hearts. We thank the women of the Co-operative Guild of Coatbridge for their kind feelings and their wish to help us in the fight we are waging against a common enemy. We are in good spirits and in spite of all the sufferings we have endured we are holding our ground. Our faith in victory is firm and unshakeable. Together with you by hard work in the rear and at the front we will achieve victory over fascist Germany."

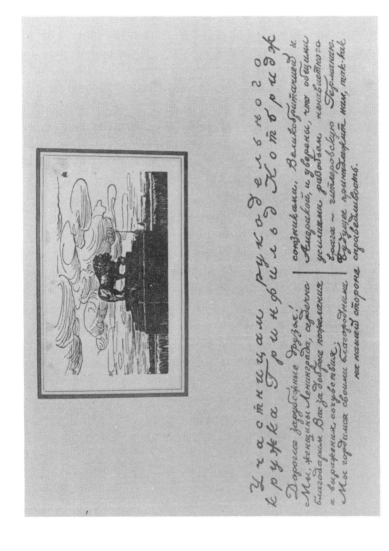

Участницам рукодельного кружка Гринвич Нотгриж

Дорогие зарубежные друзья!
Мы, жительницы Ленинграда, сердечно благодарим Вас за Вашу поддержку и выражение сочувствия к тяжёлым событиям, не оставивших равнодушными на нашей стороне | создавали. Великобритания и Америка, и уверены, что общими усилиями работаем наилучшего дела — ленинградскую блокаду. Германия будущее приближает нам, так-так справедливость.

LION STATUE ON THE EMBANKMENT OF THE RIVER NEVA.

To members of the handwork circle, Greenfield, Coatbridge

"Dear friends abroad: We women of Leningrad thank you heartily for your good wishes and messages of sympathy. We are proud of our noble allies Great Britain and America, and are certain that by common effort we shall vanquish the hated enemy, Hitlerite Germany. The future belongs to us because justice is on our side."

VIEW OF CANAL (WHITE NIGHT).

To the women of the church guild, West Parish Church Airdrie

"We women of Leningrad thank you with all our hearts for your sympathy and good wishes. We will fight together for freedom and the welfare of all nations. The annihilation of fascism is our common cause."

Прихожанкам церкви Клифтонхилля

М ы, женщины Ленинграда, благодарим прихожанок церкви Клифтонхилля за добрые пожелания.

Мы твердо верим в правоту нашей борьбы и это дает нам силы для преодоления всех трудностей, связанных с осадой нашего вели-кого города.

Мы крепко жмем протянутые вами дружеские руки и надеемся, что вы всячески будете оказывать нам действенную помощь что бы совместными усилиями разбить и уничтожить нашего общего врага.

BASE OF A ROSTRAL COLUMN.

To the women of the congregation of Clifton Hill Church

"We women of Leningrad thank the women of the congregation of Clifton Hill Church for their good wishes. We firmly believe in the rightness of our struggle and this gives us the strength to bear all the difficulties connected with the siege of our great city. We firmly grasp the friendly hands stretched out to us and we hope that you will give us all possible active help so that by our joint efforts we can break and destroy our common enemy."

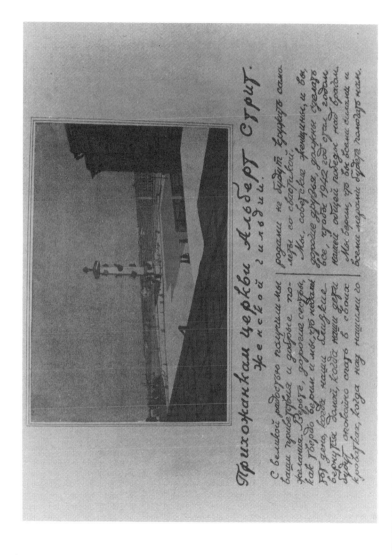

Прихожанки церкви Альберт Стрит.
Женской гильдии.

VIEW OF A ROSTRAL COLUMN WITH THE WINTER PALACE ON THE OPPOSITE BANK OF THE NEVA.

To the women of the congregation of Albert Street Church

"We received your greetings and good wishes with great joy. Dear sisters, please believe that we too firmly believe that the day is not far off when our dear ones will return home, when our children will sleep peacefully in their beds and when airplanes with swastikas on them will no longer circle our cities. We Soviet women and you, our dear friends, must do everything we can to make 1942 the year of our joint victory over the enemy. We are sure that you will help us with all your strength and in all possible ways."

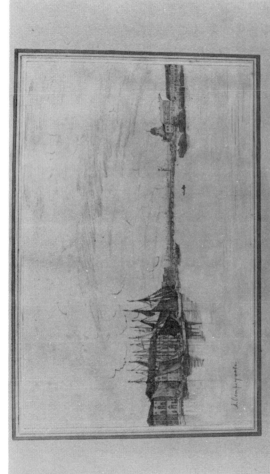

Церкви святого Фомы. Нотбридж.

Женщины Брайтмура!

Мы от души благодарим вас за ваше теплое дружеское рукопожатие и за искренние слова сочувствия, которые вы посылаете нам.

В эти тяжелые дни борьбы с ними общими врагом, мы, женщины Ленинграда, чувствуем, что вы думаете о нас, что вы помогаете нам, что вы с нами. Наша общая борьба за правое дело приведет нас к победе

VIEW OVER RIVER NEVA.

To St. Thomas's Church, Coatbridge

"We thank you for your warm and friendly handshake and the sincere words of sympathy which you sent us. In these difficult days of fighting against our common enemy we women of Leningrad feel that you are thinking about us. Our common struggle for the rightful cause will lead us to victory."

ROSTRAL COLUMN AND CENTRAL NAVY MUSEUM.

To Buchanan Congregational Church women's organisation for war work

"We women of Leningrad thank you for your friendly greetings and solidarity with us. We are even stronger in spirit and our will to victory is unswerving."

Писательница Вера Инбер

"To the women of Airdrie and Coatbridge.

We, your allies, the women of Leningrad
Send greetings to you women of Scotland.
Distance is no hindrance to you or us.
For the sake of our common cause there is no such thing as distance.

We are waging a fight against the Hitlerites over the whole continent in the wake of our husbands.
Let us speed the day and celebrate our common victory in a common language.

(signed) V.I. (Vera Inber)
Leningrad 1942".

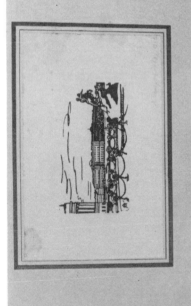

Гравюры на дереве и литографии Ленинграда.

подарены для альбома женщинам Шотландии.

Художницей
А.П.Остроумовой-Лебедевой,
работающей в Ленинграде.

1942.

BRONZE HORSEMAN.

"These woodcuts and lithographs of Leningrad were donated for this album to the women of Scotland by the artist Anna Petrovna Ostroumova-Lebedeva, who works in Leningrad. 1942".

Here is the widow of the polar explorer G. Sedov and these other ladies are women scientists.

On the corner of the 25th October Avenue and Nakhimson Avenue.

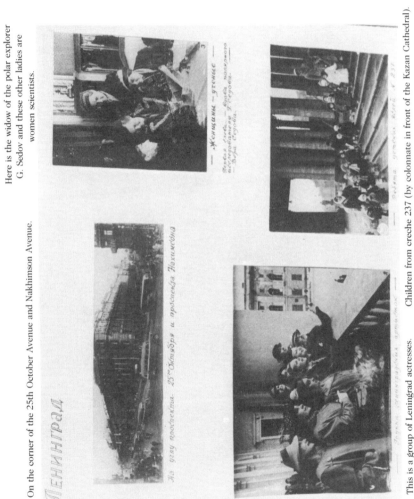

ЛЕНИНГРАД

This is a group of Leningrad actresses.

Children from creche 237 (by colonnate in front of the Kazan Cathedral).

Nina Kurganova (nurse), tending a wounded soldier on the battlefield.

Women building defences round Leningrad.

санитарка. Нина Курганова. на поле боя

Женщины Ленинграда на строении укрепление

Ленинградские женщины на строительстве оборонительных рубежа.

На строительстве оборонительных рубежи вокруг Ленинграда-

These are women drilling (Civil Defence).

Women working on Leningrad's defences.

73

Woman making tyres for lorries [M.P. Yemelyanova].

М.П. Емельянова – закатчица авторезины. Ленинграду.

Woman sailor on the ship
"Schlusselburg"
Raya Shepelova.

Рая Шепелова – Матрос на пароходе "Шлиссельбург".

Vera Yefimova, engine driver.

Вера Ефимова – машинист паровоза. Ленинград.

Housewife at her post
during an air raid alert
M.E. Shershneva.

Rostral Columns feature prominently in the illustrations of the Leningrad Album. These columns were erected along the embankments of the River Neva in St. Petersburg and in the park of the summer palace of Pushkin, to commemorate famous victories. They recalled the ancient Roman practice of sawing into pieces ships captured from the enemy and embedding their prows in victory columns.

The rostral columns of St. Petersburg also had a practical purpose. At night they served as beacons for merchant ships entering the harbour. Oil was poured into the copper cups at the top of the columns and lit at dusk, turning them into gigantic flaming torches.

The columns are 101 feet high, decorated with the beaks of galleys and figures of naiads (river or spring nymphs). The huge figures standing at the foot of the columns personify Russia's main commercial rivers, the Neva, the Volkhov, the Volga and the Dnieper.

Sheets of paper with the signatures of some 3300 women and girls were placed in large envelopes stuck to each page of the Leningrad Album. The signatories gave their names and their jobs and sometimes described their role in the defence of Leningrad. Many wrote in a shaky hand showing the effects of hunger and physical weakness; some had difficulty with spelling; a few wrote in English.

The longest lists of signatories are from the women workers at the Kirov Factory.[2,3,4]

---

[2] The Kirov Factory.

During the Second World War the workers of the Kirov Factory were famous for the defence of their workplace, Leningrad's largest industrial enterprise, as their predecessors had been for their revolutionary activity in 1905 and 1917, when it was called the Putilov factory.

[3] In 1941, most male workers had left for the Front and 70 per cent of the workforce at the Kirov factory were women, many of them young girls.

[4] On July 20th 1941, the collective of the Kirov factory issued a resolution:
"The Kirovites who are patriots for their Socialist Motherland will do everything necessary for the defeat of the enemy. Our great Red Army will receive in ever increasing quantities the armaments so necessary for the complete destruction of the fascist plague."

With the help of units of the 'people's army' the Kirov workers surrounded the factory with fortifications and production continued throughout the siege with only short stoppages although the enemy lines were only four kilometres from the gates.

The members of the first aid squad in the Kirov factory signed the album; Eva Vander, an engineer, signed. Yelena Fedorova described herself as a Stakhanovite. The Members of the workers' social club signed, among them, Jakelina Basash, a cleaner and Yekaterina Manuilova, the director of the club. Elizaveta Nikifirova proudly described herself as a Stakhanovite and like many other signatories of the album, a member of the Komsomol.

(workers of the Kirov plant building barricades).

Some describe themselves as "armed guards at the Kirov", others as or "fighters". There are signatures of an apprentice lathe operator; a foundry mechanic; packers, caretakers, a secretary, an accountant, an instructor in hygiene, a machinist's assistant, typists, technicians, a crane operator.... .

The album was taken to several hospitals including the Military Hospital no. 100, where the commandant and doctors signed, most of them in the illegible handwriting characteristic of the medical profession all over the world.

In one envelope a school exercise book with squared paper and multiplication tables on the back cover contained the signatures of a school inspector, the director of a children's home, Maria Vakhnestrova; and teachers, among them Maria Vitsenko, a primary school teacher.

Women prominent in the artistic and intellectual life of Leningrad wrote their names in the album – a writer of film scripts, Yelena Deyneke; an opera producer and acting director of the Conservatoire, Antonina Lebedeva; the director of the Institute of Oriental Studies, Maria Ovchinnikova; two ballerinas Nina Peltser and Alexandra Ushakova; a poetess Vera Arens-Takkem; and Jane Kolpakchy, a professor of Japanese at Leningrad University.

Two academic women wrote their names and designations in English – Vera Rimskaya-Korsakova, senior librarian at the Academy of Sciences and Elizabeth Bobrova, secretary of the Department of International Literature at the Literary Institute of the Academy. The envelopes also contain names of poets, critics, journalists, translators, actresses, architects and musicians, scientists and research workers.

Another envelope contains signatures of housewives who give their roles in the defence of the city – one is the leader of a civil defence group, another is in charge of an air raid shelter, some are messengers, firewatchers, instructors of air raid defence, members of house defence committees. Anastasiya Bogdanova describes herself simply as "a pensioner".

[5]STAKHANOVITE

In 1935, a miner in the Donetz region of the Soviet Union, Alexei Griogorevich Stakhanov (1906-1977), had the idea that he could increase the production of his team, if one man concentrated on hewing the coal and subsidiary tasks were allocated to other members of the team.

[6]Instead of the usual 6 or 7 tons per shift, Stakhanov began to cut 102 tons in a shift and later surpassed that amount.

Stakhanov was praised by Stalin and his efforts received wide publicity. A "Stakhanovite movement" was born and workers and individuals, male and female, were honoured for similar feats of production. The title 'Stakhanovite' could also be earned for exceptional work in professions like teaching.

[7]During the war the term 'Stakhanovite' appeared in British newspapers in praise of outstanding workers in factories producing weapons.

[8]KOMSOMOL – the Young Communists' League.

Chapter 6

Anna Petrovna-Ostroumova-Lebedeva who illustrated the Leningrad Album and supervised the creation of the album by a collective of artists was herself one of the most distinguished artists in Leningrad. Born in 1871 in St. Petersburg, as the city was called in Tsarist times, she died in her native city in 1955.

She was a painter in water colours and a wood engraver, one of the leaders of the Russian revival of creative wood engraving,[1] and one of the first members of the Society of the World of Art founded by Sergey Diaghilev and Alexander Benois. She was most famous for her series of colour prints of Leningrad from which the illustrations in the Leningrad Album were selected. In 1942, she was awarded the title of Merited Artist of the RSFSR[2]. Soon after the war she was elected a member of the Academy of Art of the USSR and received the title of People's Artist of the RSFSR. Of her many awards the one she cherished most was the Medal for the Defence of Leningrad.

The Russian Museum holds a gift from Anna Ostroumova-Lebedeva, more than 3000 of her own works and more than 300 works by other artists.

Anna Ostroumova-Lebedeva's house, where the Leningrad Album was created, still stands, 10 Academician Lebedev Street, in the famous Vyborg district, whose working-class population took such an active part in the revolutionary struggle. On the building, there is a plaque commemorating Anna Ostroumova-Lebedeva's husband, the scientist, Sergey Vasilyevich Lebedev, who discovered in the 1930's the process which enabled the Soviet Union to produce its own synthetic rubber instead of relying on imports from the Far East. The ability to be self-sufficient in this area of production was invaluable to the Soviet war effort in 1941-45. Sergey Vasilyevich Lebedev spent the last ten years of his life at 10 Academician Lebedev Street.

---

[1] Creative Wood Engraving.

Traditionally, wood engraving had been done by tradesmen who reproduced the drawings of artists. The creative wood engraver was an artist who executed both the drawing and the wood engraving.

[2]RSFSR – Russian Soviet Federated Socialist Republic.

The largest of the fifteen republics which make up the Soviet Union. For administrative purposes the Russian Federation is divided into 16 autonomous republics and a number of regions and territories.

ANNA PETROVNA-OSTROUMOVA-LEBEDEVA

The street is not far from the Finland Railway Station.[3,4] Houses were first built there in the 17th century. In the mid 19th century it was known as Nizhegorodskaya Street and several houses were built to accommodate professors and other staff of the Army Medical Academy.

When the Lebedevs came to live in the house in 1924, Anna Ostroumova-Lebedeva was already a well known artist. But the couple lived simply, devoting themselves to their work and to each other's happiness. Sometimes Sergey Vasilyevich Lebedev would lend his wife a hand by stretching canvases, sawing drawing-boards or even helping her to make prints.

Anna Ostroumova-Lebedeva wrote about their life together: "Our tastes co-incided. In our home there was to be nothing superfluous, ostentatious or showy, no luxuries, only the most essential things and they were to be simple and modest."

The Lebedevs were fond of music, literature and the theatre and their home was a meeting place for artists, musicians and writers. In their leisure time they liked to walk around Leningrad, especially when the "white nights" were beginning.

Sergey Vasilyevich Lebedev died in 1934. When the war began Anna Ostroumova-Lebedeva was 70 years of age. She had kept diaries all her life and during the siege she continued to write her comments on the day's events, in thick exercise books bound with green cloth.

On 31st August 1941 she wrote:

> *"The disaster that has overcome my country and my people is hard to bear, My heart aches for them. I would like to fly into the thick of the fighting and take the blows myself. Physically, I am already worn out, but my soul thirsts for action and work."*

Anna Ostroumova-Lebedeva's contribution to civil defence was to share fire-watching duties with her neighbours. She also wrote a great deal during the siege, completing the second volume of her 'Autobiographical Notes' and working on a book of reminiscences of her husband's life.

She no longer had her husband to lend her a hand with the practical problems of finding a corner in her damaged house where she could settle down to work:

[3] The Finland Railway Station.

Lenin arrived at the Finland Railway Station in April 1917 when he returned from exile to lead the revolution which gave birth to the Soviet state. Standing on the turret of his armoured car, he addressed the huge crowd of workers, peasants and soldiers gathered in the square outside the station to welcome him back. He taught them the first slogan of the revolution:

[4] "All Power to the Soviets"

and ended his speech with the words: "Long Live the Socialist Revolution!"

"Writing was difficult today" she noted. *"All the window panes have been broken and I had to block the windows with boards, plywood, even some of my sketches. I managed to make a little wick lamp out of a medicine bottle.*

I often write in the bathroom. I lay a drawing board across the wash-hand basin, put the ink bottle on it and the lamp on the shelf over the basin. In there I cannot hear the sound of the bombardment or the whistling of the shells so clearly and it is easier to concentrate my distracted thoughts."

On 25th September 1941, she recorded that 10 Lebedeva Street had been hit by three incendiary bombs.

On 1st January 1942, she wrote: "Terrible, merciless starvation, gripping Leningrad like pincers. We are eating carpentry glue."

In spite of her advancing years, Anna Ostroumova-Lebedeva was among the most productive artists of the war years, one of the 'real artists' as they were called, who struggled to transform the human tragedies and triumphs of the times into paintings, music or literature.

On occasions when there was a lull in the bombardment, she would take her easel and go out to sketch in the streets and on the embankments of the River Neva. One of her drawings is of a scene observed not far from the Liteynyy Bridge near her home – young boys fishing in the river, a bombardment starting up, a catch imminent, the boys too absorbed in what they were doing to move until the shells began to burst a few yards away when they – and the artist – reluctantly sought refuge in a doorway.

"Today I finished a new print – Falconet's 'Peter the Great' " she wrote. "It was done in three days. I was enraptured, passionate and thrilled with the work. To feel the tool darting along the shining board and be in control of it is a feeling that cannot be compared to anything! I had lost strength, but as soon as I picked up the tool, I immediately felt my former confidence return and my hands obeying me!"

One day in summer 1942, Anna Ostroumova-Lebedeva was taken to the office of the City Party Committee where she was shown the album which had arrived from Scotland with greetings and good wishes to the women of Leningrad. It had been decided that an album would be sent in reply and Anna Ostroumova-Lebedeva was asked if she would undertake the project with other artists. Delighted, she agreed immediately, suggesting that the work could be done in her home, at her favourite birchwood table.

CHAPTER 7

Vera Vladimirovna Milyutina, a relatively unknown artist in the 1940s, was one of the collective of artists working on the Leningrad Album.

Vera Milyutina continued to live and work in Leningrad after the Siege and she too had a long and distinguished career as an artist and teacher. She died in 1987 at the age of 84. A few weeks before her death, she sent to Scotland a recording of her memories of working on the Leningrad Album, 45 years earlier. Her first words were a message to the people of Airdrie and Coatbridge:

Dear Friends,

I am sincerely delighted at the attention paid by you to a project very close to my heart – the album sent in 1942 by the women of Leningrad to the women of Scotland in reply to the album received from them containing expressions of sympathy with the women of the besieged city. In that difficult period of the Second World War, it was their joint contribution to the cause of peace.

Thanks to the art historian, A A Bartoshevich, I was granted the rare pleasure of participating in the making-up of the album under the guidance of the famous artist A. P. Ostruomova-Lebedeva, whose beautiful watercolours, prints and lithographs made it so artistically valuable. And I am proud of the fact that on the fly-leaves of the album are the coats of arms of the USSR and Scotland, painted by me, and compositions of the Soviet and Scottish flags in the text.

I am sure that for future generations, these albums will remain proofs of the great patriotism of the Soviet and Scottish peoples, of their courage and, above all, the sincere friendship which links our two countries – the USSR and Scotland. And I am convinced that your work will be a new contribution to the cause of peace the world over – the most important problem now facing people of good will everywhere in the world.

V. V. Milyutina

5th February 1987

Leningrad (Translated by K E Birkett)

Vera Milyutina's Memories:

"After the incredibly difficult first winter of the war, hungry, cold and dark, at last the spring of 1942 came to the besieged city of Leningrad. Trees became green, the weather became warmer. But the people of Leningrad were just as hungry as before and trembling with inner cold as they had been in the preceding months of the blockade. It was impossible to get warm, even in the sun. Our legs felt as though they were made of cotton wool and our fingers would not obey us properly."

"Then on 13th June 1942 when the bombing had been replaced by artillery fire which was in turn replaced by incendiary bombs, I had a visit at my home from Andrey Andreyevich Bartashevich, an official in the Commission for the Arts. He told me that we must help our famous artist, Anna Petrovna Ostroumova-Lebedeva."

Vera Milyutina did not have far to go, Anna Ostroumova-Lebedeva's house was in the same street, as the house she shared with her grandfather.

Why did Anna Ostroumova-Lebedeva need help?

"This is what it was about" explained Vera Milyutina. "At the end of 1941, women in Scotland who were full of sympathy for the difficulties of the women in the blockaded city of Leningrad had the noble idea of sending expressions of sympathy and encouragement to them."

"On the initiative of Miss Plant and with the support of Agnes Maxwell and other women from Airdrie and Coatbridge they had compiled a beautiful album of greetings. The touching drawings were done with great care and love. The binding was of silk tartan in traditional colours of orange, white, cream and yellow across which was laid the flower of the thistle, the emblem of Scotland. In the address to the women of Leningrad, underneath the words of Robert Burns dedicated to the brotherhood of man were the words 'Your struggle is our struggle'.

"Andrey Andreyevich asked me whether I had the strength to take part in a very responsible and urgent matter – the creation of an album from the women defending Leningrad as a gift to the women of Scotland. The city committee of the Party had entrusted Anna Ostroumova-Lebedeva with it. She was to be head of the group of women asked to carry out the work".

When Vera Milyutina was summoned to the home of Anna Ostrounova-Lebedeva, it was early summer and the cold of the worst winter for a century had eased its grip on the citizens of Leningrad, but they still suffered the daily agonies of hunger and the terrors of sadistic bombing and shelling.

Vera Milyutina and Andrey Andreyevich Bartashevich, the official from the Commission for the Arts, reached 10 Lebedev Street where the artist was living with a companion, Anna Matveyevna, whom she called 'Nyusha'.

"The flat was clean and well kept" she remembered. "There were pictures and engravings on the walls...and water colours laid out on a tidy work table". But the building was damaged and the churned-up street in front of the house was overgrown with grass. The house was also threatened by the overhanging ruins of a six-storey building with a grotesquely distorted bath and bent piping visible and sheets of iron waving about in the wind.

"I was wearing my high Russian boots, having just changed out of the men's clothes I had been wearing for so many months. I was unrecognisably thin, frozen by some sort of inner iciness".

"By that time hunger had marked us all, making us hideously similar. Even though our rations had slightly increased, it was at that particular point of the siege that Leningraders acquired this quite terrifying appearance".

As well as suffering from hunger and exhaustion, Vera Milyutina had twice, through enemy bombardment, lost her home and the house she was living in had also been damaged. She had been unable to draw or paint for some time and this added greatly to the misery of her existence, since she was a talented and dedicated artist.

"Andrey Andreyevich" she remembered, "introduced me to an elderly, completely white-haired lady with a friendly and dignified manner – Anna Ostroumova-Lebedeva."

"Until then I had known about her from museums, books and exhibitions." Also present were A. F. Volkova, the artist from the City Party Committee, architect B. P. Svetlitskiy, the artist, Volina and two binding specialists.

"Now I had the chance to do real art work! Our hands were roughened by hard labour every day, we seldom had the chance to do any drawing and creative work was largely a dream."

"We started to make the album, on Anna Ostroumova-Lebedeva's favourite birchwood work-table. First she listed the problems we would have to overcome, then she told us what her plans for the book were and asked for our comments. The attention with which she listened to our comments and the courtesy with which she treated them led us to express our ideas with care and precision."

"At the time I found it very strange to be asked to discuss the creation of a collective work of art and no less extraordinary for someone as young and obscure as myself to be treated as a colleague by so distinguished a master."

"Anna Ostroumova-Lebedeva showed me, a young artist unknown to her, so much professional respect and gave me so much valuable and precious help in her capacity as a great artist that I lost my last doubts. We had to manage – that meant that we would".

"We were all finding it difficult to think. Everyone was suffering from vitamin deficiency, scurvy and anaemia. Our fingers lacked agility, our eyes clarity of vision, our brains tired easily. We were hungry, but we had no time to go even as far as the canteen to eat our meagre 'rations' (a plate of soup and a little porridge). At Anna Ostroumova- Lebedeva's request, her friend Nyusha would heat the samovar with a few bits of wood and after a glass of hot water, work went much more easily."

"I recall that one of the graphic artists, Boris Petrovich Svetlitskiy spent almost the whole of one of the 'white nights' sitting at a desk writing the text out in longhand."

"My job was to combine the design of the pages of the album into a whole, to execute the numerous graphic designs on various pages and to create the compositions made up of the flags and coats of arms of the USSR and Great Britain for the fly-leaves."

"After working for several hours and finding my eyes couldn't see any more, I would return to my bombed, partly burned-out house. My grandfather would come back from his work and we would sit down to a meal of thin broth and a galantine made of carpenter's glue and bay-leaves."

"The others working on the album lived farther away from Anna Ostroumova-Lebedeva's house than me and it was harder for them. I offered to collect grass for them but they were nervous about eating it raw."

"It fell to me to find the information we needed about British flags. Our encyclopaedia showed them only in black and white, but since we required them in colour, I had to consult the Library of the Academy of Sciences."

"I was given the necessary passes and set out to walk across the empty city, so greatly changed."

"Though I had a walking stick, I was obliged to rest frequently. I found it very difficult to get up when I had to sit down on doorsteps or heaps of rubble and to start again – for I had to cover the distance all the way from the Finland Station to the Vasilyevskiy Island."

"Suddenly behind cast-iron railings, I saw an acacia tree in bloom! I started to eat its yellow flowers, savouring the bitter taste I had known in my childhood. I couldn't tear myself away from it until I had eaten all the flowers I could pick."

"At last I reached the library. In a corridor some women were dragging a bale of books along the floor. I asked the authorities if I could see the British flags and crests. They told me that each of the library staff had climbed to the second floor, where the information was held, that day already and they had no more strength left to go up again. I explained that I had walked from the Vyborg district, that the information was needed urgently for an important purpose, but however much I begged them and showed them my pass, they continued to say firmly:" 'Tomorrow they will go to the second floor. Today they cannot do it again.' "

"The next day I set out on my journey for the second time, leaving home soon after dawn. This time I was able to work on the flags and crests for several hours in a corner of an empty study."

"In five days we had made the album, five days and nights of hard, silent work and our exhausted but happy team finished its work."

"It had grown into a handsome large book, measuring 30 by 40 centimetres. It was made up in a beautifully professional way. Its pages were decorated with water-colours, tinted and black and white prints, mainly the work of Anna Petrovna Ostroumova-Lebedeva and some other artists whose names I do not remember."

"The coats of arms of the USSR and Great Britain were exact in their proportions and colouring. They were painted in exuberant Baroque style, decorated with gold and silver, with numerous lions, unicorns, leopards, crowns, knights and shields, on intertwined pale blue ribbons, with the rose of England and the thistle of Scotland."

"On the thick linen binding of the album we mounted a fine early Russian embroidery which Anna Ostroumova-Lebedeva had selected from the reserve collection of the Russian Museum."

"We placed the album in a box-like case which we covered with a gold brocade. The left-hand pages were fitted with pouches in which we placed the sheets of paper containing the signatures of the women of Leningrad, mostly of factory workers."

The Commission for the Arts and the Smolnyy[5,6,7] authorities approved the album and it was immediately flown to Moscow. From there it was conveyed to London.

[5]The Smolnyy

The Smolnyy was the administrative and military headquarters of Leningrad during the Siege. In Tsarist times, it was a boarding school for the daughters of the nobility, established by the Empress Catherine II (Catherine the Great). In August 1917, the building was taken over by revolutionary workers and soldiers.

[6]On October 24th 1917, Lenin arrived at the Smolnyy to direct the insurrection. On October 25th 1917, he addressed an emergency session of the city Soviet in the Assembly Hall of the Smolnyy, opening his speech with the historic words: "The workers' and peasants' revolution, the need for which the Bolsheviks have stressed time and again, has happened."

[7]On the following day, Lenin's first two decrees, on peace and on land for the people, were adopted and the first workers' and peasants' government in the world was formed under his leadership. The Smolnyy became a symbol of the city where the Soviet state was born. After Moscow became the capital in 1918, the Smolnyy remained the political centre and party headquarters of Leningrad.

CHAPTER 8

The last message in the Leningrad Album was in verse, written for the women of Airdrie and Coatbridge by the Moscow poet, Vera Mikhaylovna Inber (1890-1972).

Vera Inber lived in Leningrad from the beginning to the end of the siege, with her husband, Professor Ilya Davidovich Strashun ('I.D.' as she called him), director of the First Medical Institute in Leningrad. She arrived to join her husband just before the city was encircled. The professor could have accepted a similar appointment in Murmansk in the far north of Russia, but the couple chose to move to Leningrad from Moscow, in full knowledge of the imminent danger to the city. Vera Inber, believed it was her duty as a poet to experience at first hand and to record the worst sufferings of her people.

During the Siege of Leningrad, Vera Inber produced two major works that are among the most moving literary evocations of the war years, her epic poem 'The Pulkovo Meridian' for which she received a Stalin Prize, and her diary of the siege, published under the title "Almost Three Years," in which she described, as a poet, a wife, a mother and a grandmother, the sort of day-to-day experiences undergone by the women of Leningrad during the Siege:

Vera Inber returned to Leningrad in August 1941.

On the train from Moscow her thoughts turned constantly to her parting with her grandson Mishenka – he had been evacuated to the safety of the countryside with his mother – as if she sensed she was never to see the child again.

'I keep seeing my little grandson Mishenka: he is only six months old. He left wearing an open shirt and a cap too big for him on his darling little head. He was put into a children's compartment and he lay very still, looking at everyone with bright eyes, gripping his tiny leg with his hand. I was too upset to go back and have a last look at him.'

She found conditions in Leningrad much worse than she had imagined them to be, but she was with her husband.

'My husband did the right thing in sending for me'. She wrote he always said "If war breaks out we should be together."

As soon as it was known that Vera Inber the poet had arrived in Leningrad, she was asked to broadcast on radio. Her broadcast ended with the words:

'Hitlerism will be destroyed, wiped off the face of the earth! Moscow and Leningrad will be unconquered as they have been down the centuries!'

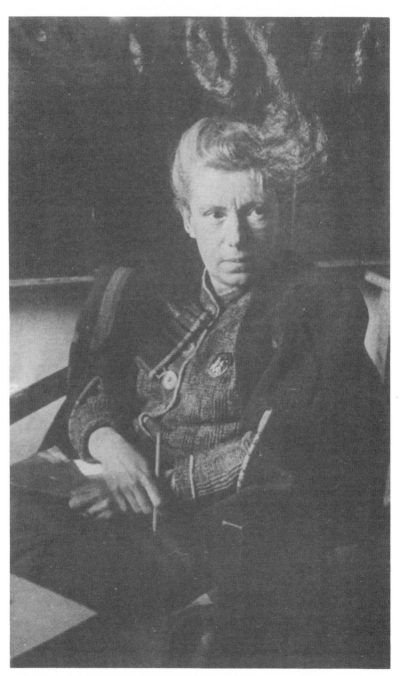

(Vera Inber, writer and poet)

These were brave words, spoken before Leningrad's last link with the outside world, the railhead at Mga she had passed on her journey, fell to the enemy. Hitler had been confident that Army Group North would capture Leningrad and "erase it from the face of the earth" very early in Operation Barbarossa.

'We shall be in St Petersburg in three weeks,' he wrote, deliberately using the old Tsarist name for the city. After the war invitation cards to the Nazi elite were found, for a banquet to be held in July 1941 to celebrate the fall of the city, but it did not take place.

As the Russian winter approached Hitler was forced to recognize that Leningrad was impregnable by military means, but he was confident that it would not be long before the city, in his own words, devoured itself. Hunger, cold, disease and constant bombing and shelling would, he believed, force its citizens to ask for capitulation. Yet there is no evidence that the city authorities were even under pressure from the public to surrender to the Germans at any time during the Siege.

By September 1941 food rationing had been introduced for all Soviet people, since most agricultural area in the Soviet Union had been over-run by the Germans. In Leningrad the situation was already desperate when the Badaev warehouses containing most of the remaining food supplies were bombed by the Germans on 9th September 1941. Vera Inber watched the flames consuming what she called "Leningrad's larder, the heart and stomach of the city."

Food Rations were cut five times more and on some days food was not available at all. At their lowest level rations allowed Leningraders the following quantities of food per day:

Dependants (housewives and the elderly)

$4\frac{1}{2}$ oz. bread
$\frac{1}{4}$ oz. fat
$\frac{1}{2}$ oz. wheat
$\frac{3}{4}$ oz. cereals
$\frac{3}{4}$ oz. sugar or confectionery

7 oz. Total 466 calories

Office workers were allowed 581 calories and children 684 calories.

Factory workers and those doing manual work essential to defence had a higher allowance, similar to the allowance of soldiers at the Front, slightly more than 1000 calories.

The authorities organised 'food search parties' made up of women and children, the sick and the disabled, to comb every corner of warehouses, ships' holds and freight lorries for anything edible.

Empty flour mills were visited and every discarded flour sack was shaken out. In breweries, spillages of malt were located below floor-boards and scooped up into containers. At the docks a consignment of 2000 tons of sheepgut was seized upon and made into an evil-smelling meat substitute. Members of a search party who came upon some grain under an enormous, empty storage tank pulled neighbouring tanks from their foundations, an operation which yielded 389 tons of grain.

Housewives cut horn buttons from clothes and dissolved them to make soup. Pancakes were made from sawdust mixed with wallpaper paste, leather was boiled and tree-bark was served as stew. Glycerine and carpenter's glue became ingredients in bizarre new recipes. Factory workers licked grease from machines and drank from oil-cans.

On display at the museum of the Zhdanov shipyards is the following document; "Please allow Comrade Gamor to leave the factory works with additional provisions of 0.5 litres of drying oil and one kilogramme of glue".

During the winter of 1941-42 public services practically ceased. First buses and then trams disappeared from the streets. In September the central power station was bombed, cutting off domestic lighting, telephones and heating by electricity. Householders used candles until supplies ran out and chopped up wooden floors or furniture to provide a few hours' house warmth. Wooden houses were demolished for fuel.

Water pipes and drainage were frozen out of action as temperatures dropped to 30 degrees below zero in the coldest winter for a century. Women and children fetched water from the River Neva, which flows through Leningrad, breaking the ice and taking home on children's sledges pots of water they were too weakened by hunger to carry.

Radio worked only intermittently, supplemented by public address systems and wall newspapers.

On 17th September Vera Imber and her husband moved into staff accommodation in the Medical Institute which was one of the main centres during the Siege for the treatment of the wounded and the starving.

One 20th September 1941 Vera Inber wrote:

Yesterday was a bad day. Fifty people were brought in here, one of them a child about seven years old. She complained that the tourniquet on her leg was hurting her. People comforted her, telling her the pain would soon ease. She was anaesthetised and her leg was amputated. When she came round she said "It's marvellous. It doesn't hurt any more". She had no idea she'd lost her leg.

As winter drew near, Leningrad was still holding out. But only a trickle of supplies could enter, arriving at Tikhvin, a railhead to the east of the city, and taken by barge across Lake Ladoga one of the largest lakes in Europe, which flows into the River Neva. As winter approached, the ice forming on Lake Ladoga impeded the passage of the few barges that escaped enemy fire. The lake was taking longer than usual to freeze solidly.

The ice was not strong enough for lorry traffic on the ice road, the motor route laid across the lake at the end of November, to be known as Leningrad's 'Road of Life'.

On 9th November Tikhvin was captured by the Germans, severing Leningrad's last, fragile lifeline.

The defence of Leningrad continued though all hope for the survival of the population had gone. A few days after the fall of Tikhvin, in desperation, the city authorities asked the people of Leningrad to attempt a miracle – to cut a new supply road, 237 miles in length through snow and ice, forest and marshland, to the next unoccupied railhead at Zaborie.

Announcements over the public address system called for volunteers and tens of thousands of hungry citizens dragged themselves to the outskirts of the city, women, girls, old men and soldiers recovering from wounds sustained at the Front.

The road was completed in 27 days with the most basic mechanical equipment and under constant enemy attack.

But several thousand Leningraders worked on to the end of their strength and never returned to the city. Their bodies lay where they had collapsed and died, shrouded and then covered by falling snow.

As the first convoy of supply trucks left Zaborie on 6th December, triumphal music by Shostakovich was played over loud speakers and actors read lines by Leningrad poets.

Three days after the road to Zaborie was completed, Red Army units recaptured Tikhvin. By the end of 1941, the Wehrmacht had lost the reputation for invincibility it had enjoyed before the German attack on the Soviet Union. In a major counter-offensive the Red Army units defending Moscow were pushing back the vast German army that had been threatening the capital. The survival of Moscow gave hope to Leningraders in the worst

(A Leningrader suffering from starvation).

Leningrad Zoo 1941 – Bomb damage to Elephant House.

(Women in Liningrad obtaining water in the street).

(Reading wall newspapers).

(Children wounded during the Siege).

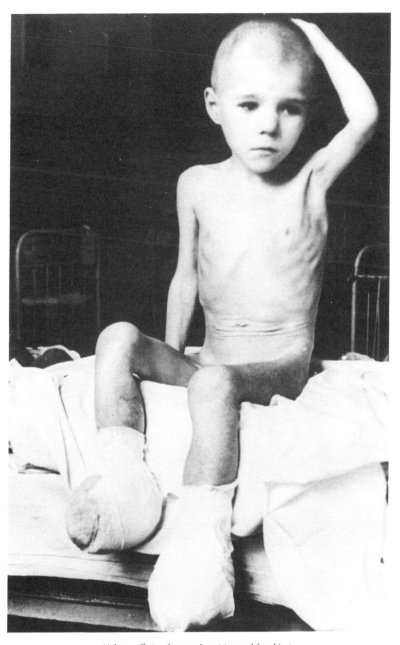

(A boy suffering from malnutrition and frostbite).

(The Road of Life)

month of the whole siege though the bread ration remained at its lowest level until 25th December.

But the bombing and shelling by German units surrounding Leningrad continued unabated. Hospitals were full and desperately short of medicines and surgical dressings:

At the Medical Institute the mortuary was also full, with the bodies of patients who could not be saved and corpses brought in from the streets. Blankets, tablecloths and curtains served as shrouds. One small bundle wrapped in brown paper and tied with string was found to be the body of a child.

In January 1942 Vera Inber wrote about a man brought to the Institute in the last stages of starvation:

"His legs moved like artifical limbs, his eyes stared as if he was possessed. The skin on his face was stretched tight. Now I know what is meant by the phrase 'gnawed by hunger'! And these desiccated skeletons are being gnawed by frost too!"

The beginning of 1942 found Vera Inber, like many others who were surviving the Siege, exhausted and depressed by the privations of 1941. Her thoughts returned again to the welfare of her daughter and grandson:

"I have had no letter from the family for so long. But how can letters battle their way through to Leningrad?"

On 9th January 1942 she heard from her daughter:

Jeanne, my little girl. Her letters frighten me more than the heaviest shelling. She writes "Misha's little face is so pretty. One can see he's not a baby now, he'll be a year old soon, but his little body is so thin and he hasn't any teeth. It tears one's heart to pieces...all the little vests and jerseys made when he was born still fit him. They're a bit short, but they still fit."

On 20th January 1942 she received another letter from Jeanne, sent in November! "Misha is mortally ill." "We gave him oxygen. He opens his little mouth for the tube like a fledgling." And on 12th February the entry in Vera Inber's diary read:

"I have just received a letter written in December. Our little Mishenka is dead. He didn't reach his first birthday." It was not until March that she heard about her grandson's funeral. "We buried him in the peasant way. We tied his little coffin to a sledge."

"I can hardly bear to read this," his grandmother wrote. "Mishenka is dead and

I don't even have a photograph of him. I must throw myself into my work to get a grip of myself."

"When the water mains burst", she wrote next, "Eight thousand Komsomol members – weak like everyone else from starvation and chilled to the bone – formed a human chain from the River Neva to the bakery, passing buckets of water from hand to hand, to enable bread production to continue."

In her diary of the Siege, Vera Inber paid tribute to the work of the young people of the Komsomol, the Young Communists' League.

The young people of the 'everyday life teams' of the Leningrad Komsomol saved thousands of lives during the Siege.

In early Autumn 1941 Leningrad had been coming to the end of its supplies of oil and coal. The only hope of obtaining more fuel was to send wood-cutting teams to the outskirts of the city. Early attempts were unsuccessful because of lack of transport and shelter for the woodcutters – mainly women and adolescents. Komsomol members took over the organisation of wood-cutting:

Working in temperatures that sometimes reached 40 degrees below zero, Komsomol teams of girls from the Smolnyy district constructed a narrow-gauge line from the forest to the nearest railway line. Then they built barracks, supplied them with makeshift stoves and in this way substantial quantities of timber were delivered to Leningrad.

Other Komsomol teams gathered thousands of pine needles and helped the city authorities to distribute an infusion made from the needles which proved to be effective in preventing scurvy.

It was also largely through the help of Komsomol teams that more than 30,000 orphans of the Siege were settled in the 85 children's homes opened in Leningrad in 1942.

Young Pioneers (10 to 16 years of age) did all they could to make themselves useful too – delivering letters from the Front, changing expired ration cards for elderly people, fire-watching, digging under the snow for edible plants, carrying pails of water from the River Neva, reading to the wounded in hospitals and helping nurses with domestic work.

(Taking a corpse to the cemetery).

Peat cutting

Loading the wood for Leningrad).

(Young Communists chopping wood).

(Girls firewatching on the roof of the Academy of Sciences.)

CHAPTER 9.

In the third week of February 1942, the ice was still thick on Lake Ladoga, enabling lorries to bring in some food. Vera Inber was taken out of the city to watch Leningrad's lifeline in operation:

'23rd February 1942.

Red Army Day! We carried gifts with us to the Front, shaving kit, fur gloves, handkerchiefs, guitars and mandolines. Some of the musical instruments were badly packed and fell out of the lorry when the road was bumpy. They cried and moaned as if they were alive.

We saw a live goat, a live dog, a live chicken. We all stared at these miracles. Beyond the lake we heard singing. We couldn't believe it! Here the people have rosy cheeks, they speak quickly, walk briskly. In Leningrad, we are pale, our breathing is shallow, we walk slowly and talk quietly.

The labour of the Ladoga lorry drivers on this worn-out, tormented road which knows no peace, day or night, is a sacred labour.

Everywhere there are notices: 'Driver have you done two runs today?' And every driver does his two journeys across the lake.'

In March 1942, Vera Inber wrote her famous lines 'To the women of the besieged city of Leningrad.'

> 'Homes without light, stoves without heat,
> Hard work, deprivation, grief and loss –
> All these are endured.
> You were the soul of Leningrad,
> Its great maternal strength.
> Nothing overwhelmed it.'

As Spring approached, all Leningraders with enough strength left to hold a spade came out of their homes to clear the streets of blocks of ice, sewage and frozen rubbish. Without their voluntary labour, epidemics would have struck down those who remained alive.

As the snow melted, corpses which had lain in the suburbs over the winter were uncovered. Some were the bodies of Leningraders who had gone out for bread and died in the street. Others lay on sledges or pieces of plywood abandoned by relatives too weak to complete the journey to a burial-ground.

On 12th June 1942, Vera Inber heard the latest news coming over the street broadcasting system – the signing of a Treaty of Friendship with Great Britain for 20 years.

"Can it be true", she wrote, "that happiness will come back again; that mankind will wake up one morning and find that Hitler isn't here any more?"

On 9th August 1942, Vera Inber was in the audience which filled the Philharmonic Hall to hear Shostakovich's Seventh Symphony – the 'Leningrad' Symphony.

Dmitry Shostakovich, the composer, had joined the ranks of the people's volunteer corps in the early days of the war. Weak from hunger, he composed the Leningrad Symphony in an ice-cold flat, interrupting his work to take his turn at fire-watching from rooftops. He rehearsed the Symphony, to the accompaniment of gunfire for six weeks – with the Leningrad Radio Orchestra, diminished by musicians leaving for the Front or succumbing to starvation. "The first violin is dying" he was told "The drum died on his way to work. The French horn is dying...". When the time came for the first performance of the symphony in Leningrad, 18 musicians were released from the Front to replace those who had died.

In September 1942, Vera Inber recorded in her diary the beginning of the gargantuan military engagement between the German 6th Army and the defenders of Stalingrad. In the second week of November they were fighting, she wrote, "for every street, every house and every staircase." By the end of the third week of November she was able to describe the start of the massive counter-offensive at Stalingrad which was to lead to the encirclement of the invaders and their surrender.

"Maybe this is indeed what they are calling the turning-point of the war", she wrote on the morning of 22nd November 1942.

Later in the day she made another entry in her diary describing a particularly heavy bombardment by a 'Sebastopol' gun. She added her own comment:

"Obviously retribution for Stalingrad."

The united efforts of the Red Army and the Soviet people in the struggle to rid their country of the vast Wehrmacht, was slowly forcing it to retreat over the very areas it had overrun and devastated earlier in the war. But units of Army Group North still lay around Leningrad with their long-range guns which were used to devastating effect whenever there was news of a German defeat on some other Front.

On 18th January 1943 the ring of German divisions round Leningrad was breached and the defenders of the city on two Fronts met.

That night Vera Inber hurried to the studios of Radio Leningrad, past the forests of red flags in the streets, young people dancing with joy, strangers kissing and hugging each other...

"This night of snow, this moonlit night", she said in her broadcast, "will never vanish from the memory of those who experienced it. Some of us are older, some of us are younger. All of us will experience happiness and grief in our lives. But this happiness we shall never forget."

In May 1943, Vera Inber was invited to read her poetry to the workers of the Kirov factory.

"They listened attentively", she remarked "though I read badly. We were in the social club which is in the basement air raid shelter. The Germans are next door, after all."

As she left she heard the sound of a waltz played on a gramophone. Two couples, girls from the fire-fighting squad wearing trousers and canvas boots, were slowly waltzing round the yard against the background of a burnt-out workshop.

"Overhead", she noticed, "a Fighter Hawk was patrolling as if protecting them in their short hours of gaiety."

The breaching of the blockade had created a narrow corridor through which a trickle of supplies could reach Leningrad. A limited evacuation of children and sick people also became possible along this 'corridor of death' as it was called, for it was regularly shelled by the Germans.

For another year the long range guns were to continue their steady bombardment of the people left in the city. One day at the end of July 1943, a boy of 14 was carried into the Medical Institute. He was bleeding badly. Both feet had been torn by shrapnel and hung in shreds.

"What a waste! I'm so young," he was shouting. "It would have been better if I'd been killed."

Two days later he died.

(Meeting of the two Fronts, Leningrad and Volkhov).

111

On the 9th August 1943, Leningrad suffered what Vera Inber described as the worst shelling of the Siege. On all Fronts in the Soviet Union, the Red Army was continuing to force the remnants of the German forces to retreat.

"The Germans are running faster than the armies of Napoleon[8]", she remarked in November.

By the end of 1943 two thirds of occupied territory in the Soviet Union had been recaptured.

On 26th November 1943, Vera Inber finished her epic poem of the Siege 'Pulkovsky Meridian' and called on her friend the artist Anna Ostroumova-Lebedeva to discuss the design of the book.

In the first week of January 1944, she witnessed a direct hit on a tram in the city centre. Seventy people were killed.

"It's still a seven-day-a-week war here", she wrote.

On 14th January 1944 the Soviet High Command gave the order for a major offensive against the Germans. In less than two weeks, on 27th January, Leningrad was liberated – by its own defenders..

28th January 1944

"Yesterday evening at 8 o'clock we had a grand salute of the kind reserved for the greatest victories. There were salvoes from 324 guns. The city of Lenin saluted the troops of the Leningrad Front. They fired rockets and the whole sky was lit up by phosphorescent light, as if a meteor had flown past. The rockets fell and burned themselves out on the ice of the river Neva. We lifted our faces towards the sky, mesmerised by this great, dazzling light."

In the United States the 'New York Times' also saluted the troops of the Leningrad Front with the words:

---

[8]Napoleon Bonaparte's Grand Army invaded Russia in 1812, on June 21st, one day earlier in the year than the German Wehrmacht's invasion of 1941. The retreat from Moscow and the final defeat of the Grand Army, destroyed Napoleon's reputation for invincibility as it destroyed Hitler's 130 years later.

"Their victory will be written in the annals of history as a kind of heroic myth. Leningrad embodies the invincible spirit of the peoples of Russia."

On 7th June 1944 Vera Inber left Leningrad for Moscow. "Farewell, Leningrad" she wrote. "Nothing in the world could ever erase you from the memory of anyone living here at this time."

CHAPTER 10

Almost half a century has passed since the exchange of greetings during the Siege of Leningrad between Soviet and Scottish women, but there are still women living in Leningrad with a clear recollection of signing the Leningrad Album and vivid memories of that tragic period of their lives which the passing years have not been able to ease.

RENATA SELIVANOVA'S STORY

"Yes, that is my signature", said Renata Selivanova whose maiden name, Renata Udova, is written in a clear hand among those of her colleagues from the Kirov factory. In 1988 Renata Selivanova was still working as a Librarian at the Kirov, the position she occupied in 1941.

"And look at that signature a few lines above mine" she continued "It was written by my mother Evdokiya Udova. We both worked in the Kirov factory at the same time. My mother was a cleaner in the House of Culture."

"Yes, I remember now. It was in the yard that the sheets of paper to be inserted in the Leningrad Album were brought to me and it was there that I signed. My mother wrote her signature in the yard too, a few minutes before I wrote mine."

Renata Selivanova talked about her early life:

"I left school in the summer of 1941 and applied to the Leningrad Institute of Foreign Languages, passed the entrance examinations and was enrolled as a student in the English department."

"When the war started, it was decided to evacuate the children of the workforce of the Kirov factory. I was asked to help with the paper-work. It was a responsible task for some of the children were not old enough to speak and without the correct documentation they might have got lost."

"Later, I was offered a job in the Library doing the work of women who had gone with the children. I accepted and have been working here ever since, except for the time when I had my baby."

Renata Selivanova looked around the large, light library with its two hundred thousand books on the shelves.

"In 1941 it was quite dark in here" she remembered. "In autumn the heavy bombardments began, a shell fell in our yard, shattering all the glass in the windows. The windows were boarded up for a time and we had to pick our way across the broken glass covering the yard."

"The librarians knew the place of all the books by heart and could get them even in the darkness. Exceptionally rarely did they make a mistake and have to go for the book a second time. The library functioned all through the war in spite of the fact that the enemy was only a few kilometres away. Those who could, came to the library or we took books to shops or exchanged them at the workplace. At times when there was bombing or shelling and people took refuge in shelters we read aloud to them or arranged discussions of books. I remember that we did 'War and Peace' by Tolstoy, "Quiet Flows the Don" by Sholokhov, and "How the Steel was Tempered" by Ostzovsky. Readers often asked for books on technical subjects or on vegetable growing."

"In winter when snow lay thick and there was no transport, my mother and I moved to the hostel. They set it up in the basement under the canteen where we were well protected. Once a shell got through three storeys but it stuck in the ceiling and did not reach us. Water pipes in the city were eventually frozen but we enjoyed the luxury of running water thanks to the plant's pumping station. More than that, we had a bath-tub in the basement so we could heat some water and wash ourselves. It was like an award.

"In spring we dug up the yard, had a pipe laid and planted some vegetables, potatoes, carrots, green peas – whatever seeds we could lay our hands on. We tended our kitchen garden all through the Summer and reaped a rich harvest in Autumn. Luckily, shells kept missing the yard, and only one bomb fell on it."

Renata Selivanova was awarded the medal 'For the Defence of Leningrad', and after the war another medal 'For Heroic Labour in the Great Patriotic War'. Her husband is an engineer at the ship-yard where her father used to work. Renata and her husband live in a two-roomed flat and their house is situated near the former front line, the place from which the shells used to be fired. Renata Selivanova and her husband are past retiring age but Renata will not leave the work she loves. Every day she takes a bus, goes along streets lined with fine modern blocks of flats and gets off at the square that she has watched come into being, formerly the site of a tram terminal. This was were she came to see her mother at work. An old willow tree with broken bark is the only thing left from those times. Her grandson often waits for her here, he is at school and comes to rummage among the books. They greet each other and together, arm in arm walk to the library.

SONYA BUGREEVA'S STORY

Another signatory of the Leningrad Album, Sonya Bugreeva, worked for 6 years in the 25th October Memorial Hospital, now in a northern suburb of the city, during the war it was in the city centre. She retired in 1983 to look after her husband, paralysed from wounds sustained at the Leningrad Front.

She pointed to her own signature and those of two colleagues, Rosenfield – the head of the department of paediatrics and Kislitsina, a sister in the Women's department who was her close friend.

Before the War Sonya Bugreeva was appointed to the post of sister in the department of surgery.

"Our head of department was a doctor of the old school" she remembered. "He never allowed us to forget our own noble mission. Working with him was interesting, but difficult. The training I got under the professor helped me to survive the Siege and save the lives of many other people."

"When that War started many well-trained nurses left to work in the military hospitals. We had new recruits – teenage girls and young women who had never worked in hospitals. We had to teach them elementary tasks – the way to move a patient, to change the underwear and sheets of a bed-ridden patient how to give injections, how to talk a patient into taking medicine. After doing our duty we regularly went to the river to fetch water from an ice-hole or to help to pull down old wooden houses for firewood. Against all the odds our department was kept as clean and orderly as in pre-war times. Our professor was the main surgeon of the city, and he demanded the same standards from his colleagues, as in his own department. We understood him."

"Throughout the war our hospital operated as a hospital for civilians only. Three very large wards with fifteen or twenty beds in each were used for those who were brought straight from the streets – victims of artillery fire or starvation. The latter were skin or bone. You could recognize the last stage of emaciation at a glance – the bluish tint of the skin, the swollen eye-lids, the puffed, mask-like face, all told their tale. These patients could not eat. Nurses sat by their bedsides for a long time trying to get down a spoonful of yeast-soup or cold water. If they succeeded there was a ray of hope, but success came extremely rarely. In most cases all attempts failed."

"It was a different matter with the wounded. They brought only difficult cases to our department, those that required complicated operations. They were often a success, but the invalids remained in the hospital for there was nowhere to discharge them in the besieged city. Many a time I had to walk long distances to get them artificial limbs. I was happy every time I brought one from the workshop."

"There is one event that sticks in my mind, when our hospital was hit by a bomb. The thick brick walls withstood the blow, only the flooring shook under our feet, the doors of the wards opened and clouds of pungent smoke rolled along the corridor. A hot sharp shell-splinter flew over my head and fell on the table. The professor, tall and thin in his flying gown, came running up to me from the stairs."

"Are you wounded? – he examined my head, hands, my back, made sure that I was all right. The shock had passed."

"That's good" he said "now start cleaning up. Calm down the patients. Let them see that nothing horrible has happened."

"His voice was calm again, strict as usual. His motto always was that the patients' welfare was a priority. Later I learned that the professor was saved by a miracle that day. The bomb fell right into his room. At that time of the day doctors used to come into his room for a cup of tea, to discuss the coming operations. The professor was just approaching the room. Luckily he had no time to open the door."

"Notwithstanding the Siege, in spite of all our difficulties, life went on. We never stopped work even in the hardest days of the winter of 1941-1942. The doctors and nurses regularly visited their patients, ignoring falling bombs and shells, climbing over snowdrifts into unlit houses and flats. With only pocket flashlights to help them find their way in. Mothers-to-be who became too weak were taken to hospital. The city was starving but in maternity homes women received some additional nourishment and the new-born were given cow's milk. To make this possible a small herd of cattle was transported across the ice of Lake Ladoga along the famous "Road of Life.""

NINA PELTSER'S STORY

On one of Leningrad's most famous statues, Peter Klodt's sculpture of a youth training horses, a bronze plaque informs us that the damage to a granite pedestal was caused by one of the 148,478 shells that fell on the city between 1941 and 1944.

A few yards from this statue stands the Leningrad Theatre of Musical Comedy, its façade decorated with a sculptured representation of the Order of the Red Banner, one of the oldest and the most prestigious orders in the Soviet Union. It was awarded to the theatre for its performances during the Siege.

September 6th 1941 was the first night of the operetta 'Masitsa' by Kalman at the Theatre of Musical Comedy. Two days later the fascists captured the southern bank of Lake Ladoga and the ring of enemy forces around Leningrad closed for the next three years. During that period the Theatre of Musical Comedy was the only theatre of its kind in the city that remained open.

One day not long after the daily bombardment of Leningrad had started, a shell hit a tram travelling along the main avenue of Leningrad, Nevsky Prospekt. First on the scene to help the injured was the First Aid team of the Theatre of Musical Comedy. Rehearsals had been immediately stopped and actresses had come running out of the theatre still wearing their stage costumes.

Leading the first aid team was the ballerina and choreographer, Nina Peltser, famous and dearly loved in Leningrad.

Nina Peltser's signature is in the Leningrad Album written in a firm hand. On another page are the signatures of her colleagues in the First Aid team.

Nina Peltser was at the same time a mother and hard task master to her dancers. Although fatigued, they had to continue to do their daily exercises, and take part in rehearsals and performances. Peltser would say again and again that regular daily work was their only salvation and she herself was an example to them all. Her temperamental dances always delighted audiences.

When the theatre was badly damaged by shells and bombs Nina Peltser recalled "performances took place in another building, the drama theatre named after Alexander Pushkin, a monumental edifice designed by the Italian architect Rossi. Shows began in the afternoon but because of repeated air-raids sometimes they had to be interrupted and resumed the next day. But the huge hall seating 1300 was always full. Seats could be booked in advance and there were queues before every performance. At factories the best workers were given tickets for the theatre as a kind of reward."

"With the coming of spring some warmth returned to the city but the large theatre had frozen through to such an extent in the course of the severe winter, that the actors still felt the cold. After two or three minutes in the theatre you felt like running away. The temperature used to stand at two degrees below zero. When people were weak and hungry, toes would go numb first. But ballerinas have to dance on their toes and we did it! Our comrades would wait for us in the wings with sheepskin coats and as soon as a dancer had finished she would be wrapped up in a coat and taken to a 'burgeuika' – a small stove made of metal. She would be warmed up and then come fluttering back to the stage in her light costume and dance on the tips of her toes, though physically very weak, just as if there were no war. In the wings many artists would fall down exhausted but on the stage all was merriment, the orchestra thundered and everything went on as it should in an operetta."

"As well as the familar productions the audiences loved, the company showed twenty new productions in the years of the Siege. One of them 'A True Story of the Woodlands' dealing with the lives and activities of the Partisans, had its debut in July 1942. Its final rehearsals were in progress when signatures for the Leningrad Album were collected."

"Gradually other theatrical companies began to be formed and started performances – for example the Blockade Theatre. In the album you can see the signature of its director – a soloist of the Kirov Theatre, N. Velter."

CHAPTER 11.

When the war ended in May 1945, the Soviet Union mourned the deaths of 20 million citizens, 12 million of them non-combatant men, women or children. Ninety-seven per cent of all Soviet boys aged 16 to 21 at the beginning of the war were dead. The Red Army, which had fought so bravely to liberate the world from fascism, had lost half its men by the time one of its young soldiers hoisted the Soviet victory flag over the rubble of the Reichstag in Berlin.

The number of victims of the Siege of Leningrad was higher than the combined total of U.S. and British war dead.[9] At the Nuremberg trials, the official figure given for recorded deaths from cold or starvation during the siege was 630,000: and for deaths by enemy fire, 200,000.

When 'VE Day' was celebrated in Britain on 8th May 1945 Winston Churchill stood with the King and Queen and the two Princesses on the balcony of Buckingham Palace acknowledging the roars of a vast crowd. Mrs Churchill was not at her husband's side. She was nearing the end of a six week tour of the Soviet Union which had included a visit to Leningrad where she met survivors of the Siege. From Leningrad she had sent a cable to her husband:-

"Think Leningrad is the most beautiful city I have ever seen."

"I found an extraordinary contrast" she wrote in her diary of her journeys in the Soviet Union, "between the serene outward beauty of this fine city and the torture to which its inhabitants have been subjected by the German siege."

She noted that during the Siege 4638 high explosive bombs, 102,520 incendiaries and 148,478 shells had fallen on Leningrad.

At the Leningrad Traumatological Institute for the severely injured she met the director, Professor Mashansky. Then she visited the Paediatric Institute and Children's Home.

"I have never been so deeply moved in my life," she wrote. "I saw quite young boys who had fought with the Partisans and were still suffering from their wounds and children who had been injured when the evacuation trains were bombed. But it lifted up the heart to see the loving care devoted to the building up of the sick and the broken in body."

Before Mrs. Churchill left Leningrad, she wrote some reflections on Russian hospitality in her diary:

[9]British war dead – 350,000:
American war dead – 250,000.

"Russian hospitality is overwhelmingly generous, but it is a sensitive and imaginative hospitality rather than an ostentatious display. It springs from a boundless desire to please the foreign visitor and to spread treasures at his feet. Russians feel happier in making gifts than in receiving them."

At the British Embassy in Moscow, Mrs. Churchill listened to her husband's victory broadcast on 8th May 1945:

"Today we think mainly of ourselves", Mr. Churchill told the British people. The following day, the 9th of May, he designated as the day when, not only in that year, but in years to come, "the sacrifices of our Russian comrades in the field" should be remembered.

It was not to be. The high hopes of peacetime co-operation embodied in the 20 year Treaty of Alliance between Britain and the Soviet Union were never realised. By the late 1940s they had been replaced by the disappointments and tensions of the Cold War.

Had it been otherwise, the women of Coatbridge and Airdrie might have got to know their sisters in Leningrad, those who survived the Siege. As it was, Margaret Plant died in 1960, her ambition to visit the Soviet Union unfulfilled and 31 years were to pass after her journey to the Soviet Embassy in London before Agnes Maxwell turned the pages of the Airdrie and Coatbridge Album again.

After the war the Airdrie and Coatbridge Album was taken to the Museum of the History of Leningrad where it has remained on continuous exhibition to the public ever since, in the section of the museum devoted to the history of the Siege. The album shares a display case with two messages sent to Leningrad at the end of the Siege, one from President Roosevelt and the other from the people of Glasgow, signed by Jimmy Welsh, Lord Provost of Glasgow.

In the 1960's, Kira Ingal, a teacher of English in Leningrad, began researching the story of the exchange of albums. The daughter of the Leningrad sculptor Vladimir Ingal, she had been a schoolgirl during the Siege and as a Young Pioneer she had worked as a volunteer in hospitals.

Kira Ingal visited Scotland for the first time in 1970. That year the 100th anniversary of Lenin's birth was being celebrated as well as the 25th anniversary of the end of the Second World War. It was also the 25th anniversary of the foundation of the Scotland-USSR Friendship Society at whose invitation Kira Ingal was in Scotland. There, at Friendship House in Glasgow, the headquarters of the society, she met Agnes Maxwell.

In 1972 Kira Ingal and Vera Milyutina stood beside Agnes Maxwell as she opened the Airdrie and Coatbridge album again, in the Victory Hall of the Museum of the History of Leningrad.

Soviet Banner of victory at the Reichstag, Berlin.

Kira Ingal

Agnes Maxwell and Vera Milyutina looking at the Airdrie and Coatbridge Album.

Fifteen years later, Kira Ingal remembered the scene vividly :

"With her husband at her side, Agnes Maxwell turned page after page and read the names of the women who had signed the album so long ago. Some of the women she still knew, others could only be remembered."

"She and her husband both wept at the sight of the album and made no attempt to conceal their emotion."

'So many years have passed,' Agnes said through her tears 'I never thought I would see the album again.'

Agnes Maxwell died in Airdrie in 1974.

"Her family informed me immediately of her death," Kira Ingal said "and I felt a great sense of loss. It was a much-cherished friendship."

The messages in the Leningrad Album to the women of Airdrie and Coatbridge were clearly a warm and spontaneous expression of the happiness felt by the women of Leningrad on learning that they were in the thoughts of so many well-wishers in far-away Scotland.

The high artistic standard of the album containing the messages was no doubt another proof of their gratitude that they were not forgotten. But the care devoted to the presentation of the album had a deeper significance.

"Now I had the chance to do real art work!" Vera Milyutina wrote in her reminiscences. "Our hands were roughened by hard labour every day, we seldom had the chance to do any drawing, and creative work was largely a dream."

One of the greatest sources of pride for Leningraders who survived the Siege was to look back and know that the city had managed to keep alive, even in the darkest days of the Siege, the musical and theatrical performances, art and literature of the city which had been renowned for its cultural life for two centuries.

Leningrad had risen above the worst the enemy could do to degrade the human spirit.

The writers and artists and composers of the Siege, Vera Inber, Anna Ostroumova-Lebedeva, Vera Milyutina, and others produced a whole body of work later to be known as the Literature of the Blockade, the Art of the Blockade and the Music of the Blockade. Their works shone with a clarity and vision that only their journey to the limits of human endurance could have revealed to them.

During the Siege scholars and architects also kept working in Leningrad. They pored over the original plans of the summer palaces of the Tsars on the outskirts of Leningrad which the Germans had occupied. They knew that restoration would be required, but it was as well they were ignorant of the extent of the destruction and vandalism wrought, until the Siege was lifted.

Leningraders grieved over the desecration of their exquisite palaces as if they were lost members of their own families.

A few days after the lifting of the Siege Vera Inber was taken to the summer palaces at Pavlovsk, Pushkin and Gatchina.

"At Gatchina", she wrote in her diary, "there used to be a granite ball on the top of a tall obelisk at the entrance to the park. The Germans had knocked it off and replaced it by an enormous swastika. But when we came to the park the swastika, fouled by crows, had already been taken down by our soldiers. It was lying at the base of the obelisk."

"At the last moment, when our troops were on the point of entering Gatchina, the Germans poured inflammable liquid over the palace and set it on fire. Sheets of flame burst out of every window, leaving a trail of black soot on the outside walls. It was as if the whole building was decked out in funeral plumes. Some of the beams were still smouldering when we arrived."

"At the front of the palace, next to the main entrance, stand two allegorical statues of Italian origin, representing War and Peace. Both remained intact in their wooden casings. The curator who was showing us around was as delighted with these statues as if they had been living people. She had hidden them in their protective coverings herself."

"On the façade of the palace are the words: 'Founded on 30th May, 1766. Completed in the year 1781.' Now one could add: 'Destroyed by the Germans in January 1944'."

"We met a man, emaciated, white-faced and dressed in rags. He stared and stared at us. Visitors from Leningrad at last! When Gatchina was liberated, our soldiers had found only about four thousand people left alive.[10]

A priority on Hitler's list of targets in Leningrad was Objective no. 9, the Hermitage, Catherine the Great's private gallery, which had grown into one of the greatest public collections of art treasures in the world.

At the beginning of the war, treasures from the Hermitage were removed to underground shelters and to the eastern republics of the Soviet Union beyond the reach of the enemy. It is recorded that as they watched Rembrandts being packed into crates, staff of the museum, "wept as if they were parting with their own children".

[10]Less than half the population of Gatchina survived the war.

Catherine's Palace, Pushkin, ruined by the Nazis.

Interior of Catherine's Palace, Pushkin.

Palace of Gatchina after the German retreat.

Damage at the Hermitage Museum.

Picture of Vera Milyutina in 1987.

Tanya Savicheva and her diary.

Piskarevskoye Memorial Cemetery.

When they no longer had the strength to walk from their homes to work, many of the staff made the basement of the Hermitage their living quarters. There were still more than a million art treasures in the vaults to be guarded.

Famous artists struggled to get to the Hermitage to record for posterity the damage done to the building by shells and bombs, to sketch the bare walls and empty display cabinets. Among them was Vera Milyutina.

A year after her death, Vera Milyutina's 'Hermitage Collection' was shown at a memorial exhibition of her paintings in the gallery of the Leningrad Union of Artists on 27th January 1987, the 43rd anniversary of the lifting of the Siege.

At a reception on the opening night, in the presence of her husband, Alexander Semenovich, one person after another rose to offer reminiscences about her life and to pay tribute to her artistic achievements.

There were warm words of appreciation from members of the artists' union whose early talents had been nurtured at the school for amateur artists she founded in Leningrad.

At the end of the evening, one of her pupils came forward with a note Vera Milyutina had written to her on 23rd October 1943. The address was 'Leningrad – the Front.'

"We need real art, art which makes one's heart sing, which makes one so happy one floats above the earth. Colour and sound blend and fill the world.

The hard, terrible times will pass away.
Life will be easier!"

On January 26th 1945, the Praesidium of the Supreme Soviet of the USSR awarded Leningrad the country's highest award for bravery, the Order of Lenin.

The medal 'For the Defence of Leningrad' was awarded to 355,000 adults and 15,000 children.

In the Piskarevskoye Cemetery in Leningrad, almost 470,000 civilian and Red Army defenders of Leningrad are buried side by side. In the little museum at the gates of the cemetery, the diary of eleven year old Tanya Savicheva records the death in the Siege of six members of the family.

Z – Zhenya died 28th December, 12.30 in the morning, 1941.
B – Grandmother died, 25th January, 3 o'clock, 1942.
L – Leka died, 17th March, 5 o'clock in the morning, 1942.
D – Uncle Vasya died, 13th April, 2 o'clock in the morning, 1942.
D – Uncle Lesha, 10th May, 4 o'clock in the afternoon, 1942.
M – Mama, 13th May, 7.30 am, 1942.
S – The Savichevs have all died. Only Tanya remains.

For many years, it was thought that Tanya herself died in Leningrad. In fact, she was evacuated to Children's Home no. 48 in the village of Shakhty in the Gorky area. But her illness, chronic dysentery, did not respond to treatment and she died in the children's home in the summer of 1943.

As Tanya recorded, all her relatives living in Leningrad during the Siege died of hunger, but another brother and sister had been in the country beyond the enemy lines when war broke out. Mikhail Savichev, her surviving brother fought with the partisans.

In 1944 Nina Nikolayevna Savicheva, her sister, returned alone to the family home. In a box, lying beside her mother's wedding dress, she found her little sister's diary.

On May 9th 1960, the 15th anniversary of the victory over Nazi Germany, a memorial wall was unveiled at the Piskarevskoye Cemetery.

On the granite stone behind the statue 'The Motherland', these words are written:

NOTHING IS FORGOTTEN.

NO ONE IS FORGOTTEN.

end